Something Greater:
The Blueprint for Overcoming Sexual Addictions

Hey guys,

Thank you for being great friends. We love you both dearly. I hope reading this book blesses your life as much as writing it has blessed mine.

Jaron J. Rice

The story you are about to read is true. Most of the names have been changed to protect the guilty.

To Jess,

Thank you for staying on me and pushing me to do this. Without your love, determination, and dedication, I wouldn't have had the focus and clarity to achieve such an insurmountable feat. Words cannot begin to express how much your love and friendship have meant to me over the years. I love you with all that I am.

Table of Contents

Act III: The Great Escape

Foreword:

I met Jaron Rice in the summer of 2004 when he and his family made the decision to call me Pastor (their earthly shepherd) and sit under my leadership. I later had the pleasure of meeting Jessica, his wife, in 2007 while the two of them were still dating. In the fall of 2008, they stood before God, their parents, and myself in my office as I pronounced them man and wife on a cloudy September morning.

When I first met Jaron, I never knew or could have imagined some of the things he was struggling with as it related to his sexual purity. But, I know that God has a purpose and a calling for every one of His creations. I later learned that the challenges Jaron faced as a child and a young man built the strength and character that would be needed to fulfill God's call on his life.

As Pastor of Spirit of Faith Christian Center and President of FICWFM (Fellowship of International Christian Word of Faith Ministries), I've had the opportunity to meet and teach people in all walks of life. I've told my listeners many times that if they knew better, they would do better. When it comes to the issue of sexual purity, too many Christians fall into the trap of believing Satan's lies. They don't understand the damage that consuming pornography causes. Even worse, they don't understand the steps necessarily to overcome this kind of behavioral addiction. They don't know any better, so they can't do any better. But that's all about to change.

When I read Something Greater: The Blueprint for Overcoming Sexual Addictions, I rejoiced. I rejoiced because I could see the fruits of my labor being manifested in one of my sheep. I saw the transformation in his life. I also rejoiced because I could see how this information would help to set others free if they apply the principles outlined in the book. The Bible says in Hosea 4:6, My people perish (or are destroyed) for lack of knowledge. The enemy has used man's natural weaknesses and ignorance to enslave him. By keeping a person in bondage, Satan has effectively nullified their God-given destiny because they will never live to their full potential when they're enslaved to a lifestyle of habitual sin.

If you or a loved one has been affected by sexual sins like fornication, masturbation, adultery, and/or pornography, then this book is for you. It takes the principles straight from God's Word and lays them out in a clear, concise instruction manual that is easy to follow. Don't let the devil keep you enslaved and prevent you from fulfilling God's plan for your life. Make a decision today to use this information so that you can experience Something Greater.

Dr. Michael A. Freeman
Pastor, Spirit of Faith Christian Center
www.spiritoffaith.org

Introduction:

To say that many men of God struggle in the area of sexual purity would be a gross understatement. The pages of history are filled with the accounts of those who were once walking in God's best and were led astray by their own desires. Some of these men include Saul, David, Solomon, Samson, and even modern-day men like Ted Haggard, Jim Bakker, and Jimmy Swaggart. It's easy to use the old cause and effect argument while blanketing lust as the cause, but when one digs deeper what could one say is the root of the problem – the area of compromise that allowed the devil to get his foot in the door?

Modern technology has introduced several new factors that could potentially make the battle for purity even more difficult. With cable TV, Pay-Per-View, and the many different facets of the internet, pornography is gaining an audience from those who would be too embarrassed or ashamed to be seen entering an adult video store or driving through the red-light district.

Porn has become the poison of choice. It's an issue that so many Christian men struggle with in the privacy of their own homes. For a long time, I was no exception. We try to rationalize it. We try to justify it. We try everything under the sun to make our sin acceptable. The single guys are thinking that porn and masturbation are better than fornication, and as soon as they get married, everything will be okay. The problem with this philosophy is that they're going to be entering into marriage thinking that their wives are going to be as willing, able, and or perverted as all the women in the movies. What happens when you find out she's not? You're probably going to be disappointed and frustrated. The married men are probably thinking that watching porn and masturbating behind your wife's back is a lot better than going out and *actually* cheating on her. This idea is faulty because Jesus said that who a man is can be defined by what he thinks in his heart. So technically you're not physically cheating on your wife, but mentally and emotionally you're far from being faithful.

I have been commissioned by the Creator of heaven and earth to give an unabridged account of my struggles with pornography and my own personal purity. This book will be very blunt and direct for reasons of credibility. One of the methods that Satan uses to keep men in bondage is to make them think they're the only one facing this issue. If you feel isolated, you won't reach out for help, because you don't think that there's anyone else out there who understands what you're going through. Child of God, this is not the case at all. There are countless believers who face the same issue on a daily basis, and until we open up a dialogue amongst ourselves for support, it's going to be hard to conquer this giant.

I may touch some nerves and step on some toes, when I'm giving my account. This is the raw, unabridged truth, and it may offend some. The truth about sexual addictions isn't pretty. However, when you see how deep in the valley I was, you'll understand why climbing out was such an accomplishment. If you're feeling convicted about something because you faced a similar situation, take a minute to pray about it. God is pleased with your decision to address your sin and repent. He will give you the grace and mercy to overcome, but you must be sincere about your desire to change. You must also keep your focus on Him. Soon, you'll see and understand that God has called us to Something Greater.

Act 1: My Story

Chapter 1: In the Beginning

My story begins in a quiet suburb of Maryland called Columbia. Columbia is a planned community that looks like one of those cookie cutter communities you see as the setting for those poorly acted and directed teenage love stories that use the late twenty-something actors and actresses to play the high school jocks and cheerleaders. This is my home. This is my life. Our house was on Farewell Road. That's another thing about Columbia. It has the stupidest street names in the entire country: Farewell Road, Bird Race, Twenty-Year Chase, Greco Garth, Jacob's Ladder, Sinbad Place, the list goes on and on. If you know the area, you'd understand.

Most of my childhood was happy. I have great parents. My father is a Pharmaceutical Rep, and my mother is a teacher. Their combined income put us comfortably in the middle class. We had a nice house, nice cars, and took nice vacations. Both my sister and I went to private school. We had what most people would call the good life, but things aren't always as they seem.

My first friend's name was Jack. He had a good-heart, but was a little misguided. His father was killed in a car accident when he was a baby, and his mother was left to raise him on her own. Our lives were very different. As a child, I envied him. My parent's weren't overbearingly strict, but there was definitely structure in our household. When I was out of line, I was spanked. Period. Jack, on the other hand, didn't get spanked. He didn't get punished. He did what he wanted. I thought it was pretty cool. He spoke to his mother any way he felt like, and she pretty much allowed it. I remember one time I decided that I wasn't going to let my parents boss me around anymore. I was going to stand up for myself the way Jack did. I don't even have to tell you what happened. Let's just say that on a 1-10 scale of stupidity, one being smart and 10 being stupid, this was a 37. Next to riding my tricycle down the steps, it was probably the dumbest thing I've ever done.

At a very young age, a girl in the neighborhood who used to baby-sit me took advantage of her authority. Her name was Kristen, and her parents lived in the house right behind Jack. I can't even begin to tell you how old I was – simply because I have no idea. If I had to guess, I would say I was 5 or 6. It was definitely a repressed memory. I was 26 years old when I first started recalling bits and pieces of the incident. Honestly, I don't remember all that much. I remember us lying on the couch together and her pressing my face between her breasts. I remember it being hard to breath because my head was under her shirt or under a blanket or something.

When I was around the age of ten, one of my mother's students became our regular babysitter. My parents were doing Amway in addition to their full-time jobs, so they had meetings in the evenings often and traveled frequently. Her name was Eliza. I liked her. She was funny, and she let me stay up late. She was really pretty as well. I had a crush on her. Sadly, that crush turned to hatred when she violated me. I was right at the age where females piqued my curiosity, but I was too young to really have any idea what was really going on. At school when people were a "couple" it meant that they held hands on the playground when the teachers weren't looking. My crush on Eliza meant I wanted to hold her hand and kiss her on the cheek at best. She had much more malicious plans in mind for me.

To be honest, I don't really remember very much about the abuse. It took me a long time to cope with it as an adult because I felt responsible. I didn't want to do what she wanted me to do, but as it happened it *felt* good. Over time, the things that I once hated, I learned to enjoy. The only reason it stopped is because my parents deemed me old enough to stay home by myself and watch my sister.

The experience opened the door and left me vulnerable to the snares of pornography. As most young boys, I had a natural curiosity for the female body, but my experience with a real life female left me hurt, shocked, scared, excited, and curious all at the same time.

Jack was fourteen months older than I was. I remember that one of my earliest encounters with pornography came after Jack's Bar Mitzvah. Because he was now a "man," his mother got him his own subscription to Playboy. This boosted his neighborhood popularity status amongst the boys like you wouldn't believe. From that day forward, I always found a reason to be at his house. If that wasn't enough, his mother considered me family, so she was very comfortable around me. It wasn't uncommon to walk past her bedroom only to see her in some state of undressed with the door wide open. In addition, his mother managed to get one of those illegal cable boxes that allowed the user to access all the pay channels without actually paying for them. You name it; he had it – HBO, Cinemax, Spice, and The Playboy Channel. The devil was setting up a trap that would ensnare me for many years to come, and I eagerly walked right into it. For a horny, curious tween (pre-teen), Jack's house was the place to be.

Over time, things got progressively worse. One day on our way home I saw something underneath a pile of leaves at the entrance of the main driveway that caught my attention. It was autumn and it was starting to get dark outside, but it wasn't late. I was in the car with my family. I looked around and it didn't seem like anyone noticed it. I lived off of a long driveway that had four houses connecting to the long driveway. Each house had its own individual driveway that connected to the main one. The magazine was lying on the street at the entrance of the main driveway. Once we got to the house and got situated, I told my parents I was going outside to play. I had to go investigate. As foolish as it was, I was *praying* that it was a discarded, dirty magazine that someone chucked out of their car or something. I ran down to the end of the driveway, and sure enough it was the latest edition of *Swank* magazine. I could see the bold letters on the cover barely poking out from underneath the leaves. My young mind couldn't fathom why someone would ever discard such a treasure. I tucked the magazine under my shirt and ran to my fort as fast as I could. Oh yeah, I had a fort. Every boy in our neighborhood had a fort. If you were cool you had a big fort that you shared with your best friends. If you didn't have any friends, you had a fort all by yourself. I was a cool kid. I shared a fort with a few of my friends. It was near the playground that was a couple hundred yards up the hill from my house. It was *perfect*. It sat right next to a bike path, but was completely secluded because of the thick shrubbery. I looked suspiciously in all directions, making sure I wasn't followed. Then I eagerly ducked inside. Behold, my sanctuary. It was big enough to seat about eight people comfortably, and a bike or two. My friends and I had hollowed out the inside with saws and hedge clippers so we didn't have branches in our faces all the time. We used old logs as seats, and arranged them in a circle. There was also a platform in the center for bottle spinning, when we were lucky enough to entice a girl or two to join us in our domicile.

I pulled out the magazine, made myself comfortable, and began to soak up all of the images in front of me. If my memory serves me correctly, this was my first taste of hardcore porn. I would watch the Spice channel at Jack's house. They would show people having sex, but never showed penetration. This was different. There was nothing hiding among these photos. I had never seen anything like this before – so raw, so *in your face*. I liked it, but part of me was appalled, and not in a good way. However, I couldn't stop looking. It was getting darker by the minute, and I knew I was going to hear my mom calling for me shortly. I unzipped my jeans and began to masturbate.

Pause. At that point in my life I was masturbating daily. I had learned sometime earlier when Jack let me watch him masturbate before volunteering to do it to me. I remember that I was spending the night at his house and we stayed up late watching *Body of Evidence* on HBO. That was my first orgasm. I was 11 years old. *Play.*

As if reading from a cue card, my mom called me right as I finished. When I heard her calling me, I thought about my precious magazine. There's no way I would even think about sneaking that into my parents house, but if I left it outside it would eventually get rained on and ruined. I could take it to Jack's house and let him keep it for me, but he had all the porn he could stand, and this was *mine.* I didn't want to share my treasure with him. Then it hit me. It was a stroke of genius. I took my jacket off and left it in the fort with the magazine. Then, I headed home. I knew my mother would ask me where it was, and that would give me the perfect opportunity to come back outside and bring some grocery bags in an attempt to make a waterproof cover for my precious treasure. My plan worked out flawlessly. I was so excited I could hardly sleep that night. I finally had my own dirty magazine, and it was about as dirty as my young eyes could stand at that point.

To say things got worse over the years would be an understatement. When I say it got worse, I'm talking about the consumption that led to my addiction. In my young mind things were getting better. I had more access to pornography. Jack's collection kept growing and growing, while my one magazine got confiscated by a friend's mother when he decided to take it home one night. But, I didn't mind too much. Jack was never apprehensive about sharing. After Eliza, my first voluntary sexual encounters were with Jack. When things first started out we would just masturbate in front of each other or take turns jerking each other off. Over time it progressed to oral and eventually anal sex. I had a lot of questions about my sexuality at that point, as you can probably imagine. I certainly didn't want to consider myself gay. After all I still liked and was aroused by females. But, I was having frequent, regular sexual encounters with another guy. For me, the idea of kissing Jack or being romantically involved with him made me want to throw up. But the sexual aspect of our *arrangement* was appealing to my flesh. I'm pretty sure he felt the same way, although we **never** talked about it. We just did it.

One summer when I was about 14, Jack told me that he and his mom were going away for ten days and he needed me to feed his gerbil. He gave me a key and everything. That was probably the best news I had heard up to that point in my life. If the old wives tale about masturbation causing blindness was true, I would've lost my sight by the second day of his vacation. Not only did I have a chance to feast on all the porn I could stand, I also had a chance to be nosey and snoop around. I had the house to myself. Jack had a waterbed, and there was a nice wooden frame that went all the way around the bed. There were drawers along the bottom, and the porn stash was in the far drawer closest to the head of the bed. Instead of just opening the drawer and pulling out a tape, I took out the entire drawer. I wanted to see all of my options in their full glory. So I set the removed drawer on the bed and began searching through the video titles. At this point I was on my knees leaning over the edge of the bed. I happened to glance down to where I had removed the drawer from and something caught my eye. I had to investigate. I retrieved the item and looked at it curiously. I looked like a videotape, only smaller. Then I realized that it was a mini cassette that goes to his video camera that he got for his birthday. Immediately I was fascinated by the possibilities of what was on this cassette. What could it be, and why would he go out of his way to hide it? I started looking around the room for the video camera. Eventually I found it in the closet. I pulled it out of the carrying case like a child opening his most anticipated present on Christmas morning. I yanked the AV cables from the bag, plugged them into the TV, then connected the other end to the camera. When I pushed play, what I saw astonished me. In front of my eyes was a homemade movie that Jack and his girlfriend Christina had made at some point. I hit fast forward and realized that the entire tape was full of their homemade adventures. From then on, I started to admire him. Sure, he was cool before this, but this was another level of cool. I hadn't voluntarily gotten beyond kissing a girl, and here he was, not even old enough to drive, making amateur porn movies . Those homemade clips occupied my time for the remainder of his vacation.

I'm not exactly sure how the issue came up, but after a while it was apparent that Jack knew that I knew about the tape. He didn't care that I knew, but he didn't want Christina to find out. So, it became our secret. Sometime later, I was hanging out with the two of them in his room watching TV. My being the third wheel was quite a regular occurrence with the two of them. I was sitting on the end of the bed with my back to them while I was looking at the television. They were lying on the bed making out and giggling. I could feel the water bed moving back and forth. He had his *Best of the Eagles* CD in the player with *Hotel California* on repeat. We were way too young to remember that music firsthand, but Jack's mom was a bit of a hippie, and she turned him on to it. After a few minutes I realized that their giggling turned into heavy breathing. I turned around only to find both of them were removing clothing as if preparing to have sex while I was sitting there. I didn't know how to react. I didn't want to stare and act like I had never seen anything like that before, but in all honesty I hadn't. I gave up. I stared. I figured if they would do that with me in the room, either they wanted me to watch or they didn't care. Jack looked over at me and gave me a nod of approval as if he were telling me to join. I was nervous but excited. Seeing things on movies is completely different than actually participating in them. I approached them with fear and excitement, like a squirrel trying to take a tasty treat from a stranger's hand. But, the excitement was short-lived. She gave the initial approval but seemed to change her mind as the enormity of what she was about to do caught up with her. Suddenly, she jumped out of bed knocking Jack to the floor, grabbed her clothes as fast as possible, and darted out of his room. I could hear her stumble down the steps and burst out the front door, slamming it behind her. I looked out the bedroom window to see her running down the driveway half-naked. Jack was running after her. I was confused. What just happened here? As I was struggling to comprehend what was going on, I started putting my clothes on. When I left the house, I saw the two of them outside talking. She was crying. I didn't know what to say to console her, and being that Jack was her boyfriend, I figured that should be his job. I started walking in the other direction back to my house, and I overheard her saying something about feeling like a whore. I went home, and I cried. I felt dirty. I was upset about what had happened, but I was also scared about what she could have accused us of doing. I wanted someone to talk to, but I couldn't in a million years see myself going to my parents with that kind of information. Needless to say, Jack and Christina's relationship ended that night. I felt responsible. I later found out that Christina got heavy into drugs, dropped out of high school, and got pregnant. Again, I felt responsible. I was starting to learn that my actions were greater than myself, and what seemed to be a harmless sin was starting to manifest itself in my life. But, this was only the beginning.

Pause. It's easy for me to view my past mistakes in hindsight and evaluate how those mistakes affected my life. But, I never really thought about what Jack's life was like. As you're about to find out, we moved away a short time later. After that, our friendship kind of died. It's not that we disliked each other, but our paths just went in different directions. He had as much, if not more exposure to porn that I did, and I know he had a lot more sex. Sometimes I wonder what things were like for him in college and beyond. He got married, and bought his childhood home from his mother. Now, he lives there with his wife and young son. I've always wondered how his addiction affected his relationships. Maybe one day I'll have the courage to talk to him about it, but for us it's been a lot easier to pretend the past doesn't exist. Now, where was I? Ahhhh, yes. *Play.*

Chapter 2: Slippery Slope

Towards the end of my freshman year of high school, my parents decided that they wanted to move to the other side of Columbia. I had mixed emotions about the transition. I was excited about having a new house and going to a new school. I spent my freshman year at a Catholic high school for boys. I hated every minute of it. One of the teachers that held class across the hall from my English class was arrested towards the end of the year for having inappropriate and illegal relationships with his students. It was kind of exciting to see the police come and arrest him, but at the same time, I was disgusted by the stereotypical sexual abuse linked with the Catholic church. Moving to another house in another neighborhood would give me a fresh start at a new school. I was looking forward to it. For the first time in my life, I was going to public school.

I liked my new school. I was fairly popular – not only because I played varsity football, but because I was smart and funny. I was continually amazed at some of the clothes that I would see some of the girls wearing. I would watch girls arrive to school in one outfit and walk straight to the bathroom to change into something more revealing that their parents wouldn't let them leave the house in. This was culture shock for me. I spent ten years of my life at a small private Christian school with the same girls in my class all ten years. Then, I went to a boys' school for my freshman year. This was the first time in my life that I was exposed to females in this kind of abundance.

It took a while for us to get settled into our new house. My parents had the house built to their specifications, so when I say new house, I really mean it. We moved in a few days after Thanksgiving in 1997. Along with the new house, my parents got a new computer and a high speed internet connection. This would begin my love, or should I say lust, affair with online porn. Up to this point, most of my visual gratification came by way of magazines or video tapes. Jack had a computer with a slow dial-up connection, so there were times we tried indulging our lust online, but there's something painfully torturous about watching a sultry image download at dial-up speeds, so eventually we stopped trying. After I moved away, the internet provided the opportunity for me to explore and indulge. I was no longer bound to what was physically available. The online experienced allowed me to satisfy every curiosity that I could've imagined.

Over time I grew partial to literotica. They were pornographic stories that allowed your imagination to run wild with all the naughty little details. I liked it for a number of reasons. First, I didn't have to be as cautious when looking over my shoulder. If I were looking at images, it's quite obvious what I was doing. But, when reading a story, all you could see was text on the screen so my parents would think I was researching something for homework. Also, I was always a creative writer with a vivid imagination, and many times the images I could create in my head were more debaucherous and sinfully satisfying than what I could view on the screen. I loved reading the older women younger men stories about the housewife and the high school kid that comes over to cut her grass – things of that nature. I think I leaned more that direction because of Jack's mom. By the time I moved away, I had seen her naked hundreds of times and secretly developed a lustful longing for her. These stories allowed me to swap myself with the young guy and her with the housewife as I would play the scenes over and over again in my head. I was digging myself deeper and deeper into the bowels of lust, but it was never enough.

That summer I took on a job as a lifeguard for a pool management company. They managed small facilities like apartment complex pools and other similar venues. I was sixteen at the time. I loved the job. Not only was I in a position of authority, but I got to sit in the guard chair with my dark shades on and soak up all the girls in bikinis when I was *supposed* to be watching the water. It's a miracle that no one ever drowned on my watch, because I probably wouldn't have noticed.

One day I was working at the pool when these two girls came in. I later learned that they were sisters – Kat and Marie. Kat was younger than I was at the time. She was only fifteen, but she looked like a full-grown woman. I hated how loud she was. She was white, but she swore she was black in a previous life. She only fooled around with black guys and took pride in her "ghetto booty." Actually, she'd fool around with *anyone,* if the price was right. She wasn't pretty, but she wasn't ugly either. She didn't have a boyfriend, because no one wanted to date her. All of her male friends, including myself, just wanted to get laid. She had bleach blonde hair with her bangs dyed pink, dark mascara, and a lip ring. I mean seriously, who wears mascara to the pool?

Her sister Marie was the complete opposite. She was tall and quiet. Marie was eighteen at the time and just finished high school. She had long hair and even longer legs. She was taller than me, and I stood close to six feet at that point in time. If I had to describe her in one word,

I would say she was homely. If she put on some makeup and took off her baseball cap, she would actually look pretty good. To say she was a tomboy would have been fitting. One day during my lunch break, we walked across the parking lot to the basketball court to shoot around. I should've never challenged her to a game of one-on-one. I didn't recognize the signs – the boyish attire, the height, the baseball cap. This girl was an *athlete* in every sense of the word. Needless to say I got whooped, and to borrow a line from the great Forest Gump, "And that's all I have to say about that."

As the summer progressed, Marie and I became closer. She was like my homeboy more than anything. I later learned that she considered herself a lesbian and had quite the taste for women – another thing that we both had in common. I'm not exactly sure how things started down the sexual path, but I know some playful suggestions were involved. I used to joke that since I was a virgin (well, I had never had sex with a female), and she'd never been with a man, that we should hook up and do each other a favor. She would laugh gingerly, as if embarrassed, and then pause and sit in silence looking off into the distance as if actually considering the offer. I persisted over the next few days until she finally gave in. The day was July 4th, 1998. At this point I didn't have my license. In fact, I was scheduled to start taking Driver's Ed the following month. So, my mom would bring me to work in the morning and pick me up in the evening. Sometimes I would stay late and go back to Marie's apartment and tell my mom to pick me up later. That night was no exception. I told my mom that I was going to watch the fireworks after work with some friends, when in actuality I was planning on creating some of my own.

That day I could hardly sit still or focus on anything. For a sixteen year old boy, the anticipation of having sex for the first time is the ultimate distraction. I looked at the clock every three minutes and cursed it for moving so slow. After what seemed like nineteen hours of working, eight o'clock finally rolled around. For a hot, tired lifeguard there are few things sweeter than closing time after a long day. Marie walked over to me and asked me if I was ready. I told the other lifeguard that I had some "business" to attend to and that he'd have to clean and lockup himself. We started walking up the street towards her apartment. My heart was beating so hard in my throat that I felt like a hard cough would cause it to spill out onto the concrete. The excitement and anticipation that I felt all day had transformed into sheer terror. I was scared. I started thinking of excuses for why I couldn't go through with it, but my mind was drawing a blank. I couldn't just come out and tell the girl who had previously kicked my butt in basketball that I couldn't have sex with her because I was afraid. I had been emasculated by her once, and I don't think my pride could handle that once more.

We arrived at the apartment to find it empty. Her mom was out with her friends celebrating, while her sister Kat was undoubtedly in the middle of some random act of debauchery in the backseat of someone's car. She led me back to the room she shared with her sister in the small two bedroom apartment. The room was an absolute mess. It looked like her clothes hamper threw up, and the smell was enough to turn my stomach. I looked around to see what could possibly be producing such an unnatural odor only to find a cage in the back of the room housing a couple of ferrets. She started undressing. I stood there and stared. I felt so awkward. By the time she was completely naked, I had only managed to take of my flip flops and loosen the draw string to my swimming trunks. She came over and helped me, then violently pushed me down onto the bed. Here I was about to be violated by a woman bigger and stronger than me, not to mention better at basketball. All the pornographic education in the world couldn't help me now. This was the real thing. I felt like I was on a rollercoaster about traverse the first big dip. I closed my eyes and hoped for the best.

When we finished, I wanted to cry. Not only had I surrendered my virginity to a lesbian, but I was completely disappointed with the experience. It reminded me of the time I went fishing with my friend and his uncle, and I tasted beer for the first time. I was so upset that it was disgusting. The commercials made it look so good. That's what having sex was like. I had such lofty expectations. This was *nothing* like the sexual encounters I had seen countless times in the movies. They made it look so easy. This was hard. I had no idea what I was doing. Women in porn movies seemed so vocal, like it was the greatest thing in the world. Maybe I wasn't doing it right. We had sex a few more times that summer, but each time was more disappointing than the last. I was thrown for a loop when she started showing affection in public like we were a couple. That definitely wasn't part of the plan. I tried to let her down easy, but the plan blew up in my face. Once again, my actions had consequences that went beyond myself.

In August I started taking Driver's Ed classes. Our classroom instructor was an old African guy with a thick accent. No one really understood what he was saying, so we didn't really pay attention. I sat in the back of the class eyeballing the femininas. I saw a pair of girls huddled together to my left giggling. It looked promising, so I scooted my desk over towards them. Their names were Sonja and Alicia. Sonja was Persian, but she was adopted by a white family. She's what I like to call "westernized." Alicia was an All-American blonde hair, blue-eyed gal. If Sonja weren't so incredibly hot, Alicia would've had no problem holding my attention, but at the moment, she was the less attractive of the two.

For the remaining weeks of our classroom training, I sat with the girls. Towards the end of the class session, I tried to muster up the guts to ask Sonja for her number since she went to a different school, and I probably wouldn't be seeing her once class was over. But alas, I had a better idea. I decided that I'd express my interest in Sonja to her friend Alicia and have her put in a good word for me. I know it sounds pretty lame, but give me a break; I was sixteen. At the time it seemed like the logical thing to do. It was a way for me to express my interest indirectly; that way if she wasn't interested in return, I wouldn't have to deal with the rejection face to face. I gave Alicia a note to give to Sonja that told her of my interests and left her my phone number and my e-mail address. I thought the plan was flawless. However, I didn't take into consideration the possibility that Alicia herself might've been interested in me and would've gone out of her way to derail my plan in a selfish attempt to gain my affection. I'm not a fan of Murphy's Law, but it seems to be quite fond of me.

The next day I got an e-mail from none other than Sonja's friend Alicia. The first few sentences were blunt and to the point. She told me that Sonja wasn't interested, but that I shouldn't be discouraged because I'm a great guy and should have no problem finding a girlfriend and blah blah blah. I knew where it was going before she even finished the e-mail. I knew she was going to ask me out, so why did she have to write a five thousand word essay dancing around the subject. Seriously, if I wouldn't read Shakespeare when my grade depended on it, there's no way I'd spend the amount of time necessary to read the romantic ramblings of an adolescent girl. I skimmed over the e-mail looking for her phone number so I could give her a call. She wasn't my first choice, but I figured 2nd place wasn't so bad after all. I mean hey, it's better than being alone right? At least that's what I thought at the time.

One evening in late August, I went out on the deck to put the cover back on the grill. It was about an hour or so after we had eaten dinner, and it was already dark outside. I stood there for a minute to let my eyes adjust to the darkness. As I struggled in the dark to find the opening on the cover, I saw a light go on in the house directly behind mine. My neighborhood had rather large houses, but they were too close together. This was never more apparent to me than that very moment because as I glanced up at the light that had just caught my attention, I noticed my neighbor's wife walk past the window half-naked. This must've been their bedroom. She looked as though she was preparing to take a shower. I was drawn to the site like a moth to a flame. I stood there on my deck for twenty minutes in the dark staring at the window hoping to get another glimpse of flesh. A few minutes later I got my wish.

I'm not sure why I found this so appealing. I had seen this woman in the neighborhood a thousand times and not found her worthy of a second look, but the excitement and intrigue of my first voyeuristic experience made up for that. I was hooked. From then on, I always found a reason to be outside on the deck doing *something* around that time with the hopes of getting another peek. I had come across those types of hidden camera pictures and videos online before, but I never thought I would experience them firsthand. I wouldn't have considered myself a peeping tom. I was never bold enough to go onto someone else's property to peer into a window. That seemed too perverted to me. I would rather be sitting in a lounge chair on my deck and *accidentally* get a peek at some flesh in the window.

Summer came to a close and I started my junior year in high school. I was still *dating* Alicia, but the only reason I continued seeing her is because she would let me feel her up when we made out. She was possibly the most annoying girl on the face of the planet. She had more cling than a wet pair of underwear. If we were talking on the phone and I told her that I had to go because it was time to eat dinner and I'd call her back later, she would call me back ten minutes later asking me what I was doing. After a while I figured enough was enough. I broke up with her via e-mail. I thought it was poetic justice with a touch of irony since she asked me out via e-mail. She was upset and begged me to give her another chance. I told her I'd have to think about it, even though I had no intentions of doing so. A few weeks later my parents went away for the weekend and left me home alone....for the first time. I had the house, the car, and very bad intentions. I figured I'd capitalize on my temporary freedom by inviting Alicia over. I told her that I wanted to talk about *us,* when in actuality I just wanted to have sex with her, which I hadn't managed to accomplish in the few months we dated. She was trying to win me over emotionally while I was trying to win her over sexually. I got the better end of that arrangement. Afterwards, I was disappointed. I never talked to her again after that night. Oh, she called. I just didn't answer. In case you're just figuring it out, I was a bit of a jerk.

This didn't make any sense. Real life sex wasn't as exciting as porn sex. What was I doing wrong? This is not what I bargained for. I also didn't take into consideration the fact that these *objects* that I was using to gratify my sexual desire actually had feelings and emotions. I was a child in a grown man's body. I was in over my head and couldn't swim. Just as I started sinking, God threw me a lifesaver.

Chapter 3: You Can't Run From God, Jonah

In November of 1998, my parents made me go to a weekend retreat called Manhood 101. I really didn't want to go, but they forced me so I complied. The retreat was sponsored by the same Assemblies of God church (Bethel Assembly of God) that owned the Christian school (Bethel Christian Academy) I had attended from kindergarten until the eighth grade. I can't remember specifically where we went, but I do know that it was way off the beaten path. The site had some small cabins, a basketball court, and did an excellent job of isolating us from civilization.

The time I spent at that retreat would change my life. To this day, I'm glad my parents made me go. On November 14th, 1998 I gave my life to the Lord. I grew up in a Christian home, but this was the first time in my life that God became real to me. He wasn't some lofty deity that had more important problems to deal with than my seemingly meaningless life. We became intimate with each other, and I realized that the Creator of heaven and earth actually wanted to be a part of my life. My father tells me that when I came home from that retreat, I was glowing like Charlton Heston on *The Ten Commandments* when he came back down the mountain after being in the presence of God.

Becoming a Christian didn't immediately change who I was. The Bible says that if any man is in Christ he is a new creature, old things have passed away and behold all things become new, but this verse is only true in one's life if they believe it and receive it through faith. My behavior didn't change immediately, neither did my appearance. At my core I was still me, but my heart was made new. I had a new outlook on life – a new sense of hope that transcended my flaws and a justifiably tainted view on life. I had a chance to start over, and I intended to take advantage of it.

I took my inward transformation to the extreme. From then on, I was known as a "Jesus Freak" in high school. I had a closet full of Christian t-shirts, a car full of bumper stickers, and a Bible tucked into my backpack. We met for prayer before school every morning, and I started going to Bible study on Wednesday nights. I got into arguments with my teachers because of my views on homosexuality. I wrote articles in the school paper about how intolerant our culture and society was to Judeo Christian values – much to the chagrin of the principal. I was on fire, simply put. Fewer things brought me more joy than being able to share my faith with someone. The guys on the football team affectionately referred to me as "Preach".

For the rest of my junior year, I decided not to date. I was focused. I was happy. I was doing the Lord's work. I had gotten to the point where my struggles with porn were reduced from an addiction to a casual nuisance, or so I thought. Instead of watching porn and masturbating everyday, I was *only* doing it once or twice a week. In hindsight, that is almost laughable. A person who smokes crack once or twice a week is still a crackhead. *Selah*. The problem is that lust, especially porn, is like weeds. If you don't kill the root, they'll keep coming back.

My dad always told me, "When God wants to bless you; He'll send you a woman. When Satan wants to curse you, he'll send you a woman." I guess the real question is: who sent you? I know who sent *her*. This particular "*her*" happens to be a girl named Mary Beth. She walked into my life at the beginning of my senior year. It started off innocently enough. I remember it like it was yesterday. It was a Friday in the beginning of October. We had a half day at school for some reason, and it was raining cats and dogs outside. I remember this seemingly insignificant detail because it actually plays into the story. Mary Beth lived in my neighborhood. The street I lived on was two streets off of hers. I knew that I had seen her around before, and I actually knew which house was hers. I just didn't know her name because I had never spoken to her – before that day at least. I didn't have a car at the time and was walking to school. I didn't particularly mind. It wasn't terribly far, and it gave me some time to pray. I wasn't walking home though because I had football practice after school and my parents would come and pick me up or I'd catch a ride with one of the guys. I can't quite remember what was going on with the half day, but I remember being happy because we didn't have practice that day, even though there was a game the next day.

I was standing in the hall talking to a couple of my friends when I saw Mary Beth walking towards the exit. An idea struck me. Maybe I could ask her for a ride home since we lived so close to each other. I walked over to her and introduced myself. At that point in my life I only got shy and awkward around *really* hot girls. Mary Beth was decent looking, but she wasn't a knockout. I remember thinking that if she lost some weight she'd be gorgeous – not that she was fat, she just wasn't thin. Some people know how to dress their size. Unfortunately, she didn't. She had convinced herself that she was a size 6 when in actuality she was probably a 12, and all of her clothes looked two sizes too small. Nevertheless, she had a car and I didn't. I had an objective, and she had no clue. I introduced myself and told her about my dilemma – not having a car, the torrential downpour going on outside, and my fresh pair of red, suede Saucony sneakers that matched my fresh red FUBU t-shirt and not wanting either of them to get soaked. Her lack of sympathy for my overpriced and outrageously 1999 wardrobe was overcome by her fondness for my smile. She told me that she had to run to the mall to pickup something for her mom, but if I was willing to ride with her, she would gladly drop me off at home when she was done. To me that sounded a lot better than walking through the mud in $100 sneakers. I obliged, and we were on our way.

On the way there, I realized that God must've given her the special ability to absorb oxygen through her pores, because she certainly didn't take a breath once she started talking. After she got whatever it was that she needed for her mom, we decided to stop by the food court and grab something to eat. Up to that point in my life, I had never witnessed a human being inhale a Cinnabon without chewing. She must've noticed the look of amazement on my face because she volunteered that they were her weakness without my saying anything. We continued talking for a little bit, and when I say we, I mean she; and when I say a little bit, I mean for three freaking hours. Had it not been for my mom blowing up my phone wondering where the heck I was, I honestly think I'd still be sitting in the food court listening to her.

On the way home she continued making small talk, and I casually asked her what she was up to that night. She told me that she was going to be the third wheel with her friend Emily and her boyfriend that night. Then she went on and on and on about how she hated being the third wheel and how she wished she had someone to go with her so it could be a double date. "Jeese, just ask me out already," I thought. She danced around the subject so much that *my* feet were starting to hurt, and I realized that if I didn't suggest it, it wasn't going to happen. So I did, and she accepted before I could finish my sentence. She even offered to pay. "Even better," I thought. I started feeling like a trophy wife. After all, she was the one with the car and the money.

She came to get me around six. We drove to Emily's house to pick them up; then we headed over to a local Mexican place to grab something to eat. This is a public service announcement: don't ever, under any circumstance, eat Mexican on a first date. Those of you who are familiar with the digestive consequences of eating Mexican food, know exactly where this story is headed. We hadn't even gotten to the movie theater yet and my stomach started acting up. I had the BG's. For those of you who are unfamiliar with that term, BG's is short for the "bubble guts." I felt like Harry in *Dumb and Dumber* after Lloyd had spiked his drink with Turbo Lax – just my luck. To make matters worse when we entered the theater lobby my ex girlfriend Alicia was standing in line a few people ahead of us. Perfect. This was lining up to be a fitting end to a really weird day.

I stood in line silently praying that Alicia wouldn't turn around and see me standing in the back of the line. As luck would have it, even though I don't believe in luck, one of my friends on the football team walked into the lobby, recognized me, and shouted my name as loud as he could to get my attention. Since I don't believe in coincidence, it's moments like these that really lead me to believe that God has a sense of humor. I turned to see who was shouting my name, as Alicia turned to see if it was in fact that same Jaron who dumped her via e-mail, called her over just to have sex, and then never spoke to her again. Yeah, that Jaron. I was completely and totally busted. I gestured to my friend that I'd come talk to him in a second as I braced myself for the inevitable conflict that was about to ensue. Alicia left her spot in the front of the line to walk to back to where I was standing. I could see the wheels turning in her head as she was thinking of the perfect way to tell me off.

I wasn't so much worried about myself. I've dealt with irate women before. In fact, I could've written a master's dissertation on how to defuse an angry woman without being slapped, stabbed, or spit on. My biggest issues were that a.) we were in a public setting, b.) I was around people I knew, and c.) I was on a date – a first date at that. This scenario had potential disaster written all over it in the worst way. Little did I know that Mary Beth was about to step up in a big way.

Alicia: How come you can't call nobody back?
Me: Hello, Alicia.
Alicia: And who is *this*? She your new girlfriend?
Mary Beth: Not yet, but I'm working on it.
Me: Huh?

Before my adolescent brain could fully comprehend what was happening, Mary Beth grabbed the opening of my coat with both hands and pulled me in hard for a kiss. Apparently she meant business because she planted one on me that made my toes curl.

Alicia: You better watch out for him, because he'll hit it and quit it.
Mary Beth: Just because you couldn't hold his attention doesn't mean I'll have the same problem.
Alicia:<swearing, then storming off>
Me: Well alrighty then.

I think that incident changed my perception of Mary Beth. Sure, she may talk a bit too much, but when it's all said and done, I knew that she had my back. We grabbed our tickets and headed into the theater.
    The theater was empty. We went to see *Three to Tango* on opening night. Apparently everyone else knew that the movie was going to be awful except us. Emily and her boyfriend opted not to sit near us because the theater was empty and they wanted some privacy. Shortly into the movie Mary Beth leaned over and told me that she was cold. In an attempt to be chivalrous, I took off my coat and covered both her and myself up. She leaned in even closer. I looked her in the eyes and without saying a word, she was begging me to kiss her. I didn't take much convincing. What started out as a single kiss turned into a full-fledged makeout session. The first time I came up for air, I realized that we had missed all of the previews and the movie was well into the plot line. I felt Mary Beth fidgeting with my belt buckle underneath the coat. I knew exactly what she was up to, but for some reason I didn't protest. Shortly after, her head disappeared underneath the coat.
    That night, as I lay in bed, I could feel my spirit and my flesh arguing. My flesh was proud and excited about the recent conquest and the future possibility. My spirit was grieved, because I knew I shouldn't have allowed myself to lose control in a moment of weakness like that. I prayed and asked for forgiveness shortly before I dozed off to sleep.

Chapter 4: The Devil Wore My Jersey

I woke up to the sound of the doorbell at 9:00am. I normally set my alarm for 10 on game days because we had a team breakfast at a local restaurant at 10:30. I was not happy about having to wake up any sooner than necessary. I rolled out of bed and shuffled to the door in my boxers like a zombie. I swear if this was a Jehovah's Witness at the door, I was going to let them see what an offensive lineman in a pair of boxers looked like in hopes of scaring them away. I opened the door, and there stood Mary Beth. "Wake up, sleepy head!" she said. I was as dazed and confused as a Led Zeppelin song. As if sensing the "what the heck are you doing here" look on my face, Mary Beth said that she came over to see if she could wear my away jersey at the game. At my school, it was popular for guys to let their girlfriends wear the opposite jersey of the one we were wearing on the field. If you didn't have a girlfriend, then your mom wore your jersey. I went back upstairs, grabbed the jersey, came back down, and gave it to her. Her face lit up as she thanked me and then skipped back to her car. Now all I had to do was explain to my mom how she had been replaced by my "girlfriend" that I met yesterday.

My relationship with Mary Beth started on the wrong foot, and it never really got back on track. Our dates generally consisted of dinner, a movie, and a lustful escapade in a parked car. During my time with her, my relationship with God began to suffer. I was still leading prayer at school; in fact, Mary Beth started attending. I still went to church. I still did everything on the outside to let everyone think that nothing about me had changed. But I knew the truth, and God knew the truth. When I had gotten saved the year prior, I pledged to remain abstinent until I got married. I rationalized with myself that allowing Mary Beth to go down on me technically wasn't sex, so technically I had not reneged on my pledge. I became one of *those* Christians – an "anything but sex" Christian. Purity was not my focus. Instead of focusing on how pure I could be, I was more concerned how close I could get to the line without going over.

There were other factors about our relationship that caused strife – her parents, for example. Since I grew up in a sheltered community and went to private school most of my life, I was a bit naïve. When I was growing up in Columbia, I was always a noticeable minority – being black. In all honesty, it didn't bother me. I was use to it. In fact, most of my friends joked with me that I was an Oreo – black on the outside, white on the inside – because I didn't sound or act what they considered to be "black". My relationship with Mary Beth showed me firsthand that not everyone was as open and accepting as me and my family were. Her parents were not okay with our interracial relationship, so I was not allowed over her house.

When you're not truly happy in life, you find solace in habit and routine. In a way, it helps numb you, so the time passes without you really noticing. Mary Beth and I dated for about two months. Eventually, things started to unravel about as quickly as they came together. It was getting close to Christmas, and I remember asking her what she wanted. Being that I was in high school and was only working part-time, my funds were severely limited. The response I got from her wasn't at all what I was expecting. An engagement ring? Was she serious? I'm freaking seventeen years old, and she wants me to get her an engagement ring. I remember thinking that she must've lost her mind somewhere along the way.

We had to have a talk. She told me how she wanted us to go to the same college, get married, and live together. I had a sly smile on my face the entire time because I kept expecting her to crack up laughing and tell me she was just kidding. The problem is she never did. She was about as serious as she was crazy. In my adolescence, there were very few times where I had to depend on myself to be the sole voice of reason. This happened to be one of those times. I told her that I was in no way, shape, or form ready to be married. It takes a man to take care of a wife, and I had to admit to myself and to her that I was a seventeen year old boy. She was hurt. She was shocked. She thought that we would be on the same page about this. She claimed that I didn't love her. At that age, I'm not quite sure that I knew what love was, but I had gotten myself into a bind by telling her that I loved her for the last two months. The tiny snowball that started at the top of the hill was now a rolling mountain threatening my little town at the bottom. She gave me an ultimatum. She told me that if we didn't get engaged that she would have to leave me because she didn't truly believe that I loved her.

When you're seventeen, life seems so complex. But when you get older and look back, you realize that those were the times when life was simple. Though I was dealing with things way above my maturity level at the time, God had given me wisdom beyond my years. Well, He gave me wise parents who did an excellent job raising me. So, Mary Beth and I parted ways that day. It stung at first – like ripping off a Band Aid. First all you could feel was pain, and then it went numb. After a short period, I couldn't feel anything. I found out that shortly thereafter, she got engaged to another guy. My young, natural mind wanted to be jealous, but when I found out, all I could feel is relieved. The news confirmed to me that I made the right decision. She wasn't really in love with me. She was in love with the idea of being in love. She had an emotional deficiency. She was trying to find a carnal man to fill the void that can only be satisfied by the Man who died to save her soul.

That all happened towards the mid point of my senior year. After that, the rest of the year seemed to fly by. I had no idea of the challenges that would await me in college. I thought that college was going to be everything I saw on the movies – drunken frat parties, late night cram sessions, and all the hot girls I could get my hands on. I don't know if it was a conscious decision on my part, or it was just the result of my sin weighing in on my conscience; but my relationship with God took a backseat. He never left. I was the one who walked away. I never stood up and said, "God, I don't want you anymore." But at the time, the things of the world seemed much more appealing. By the time I started at the University of Maryland, there was really nothing that distinguished me from the unbelievers. I would spend the next few years of my life in that pathetic state.

Chapter 5: The Modern-Day Sodom

I remember it like it was yesterday. I was working my last shift of the summer. I was still a lifeguard, sitting up in the chair watching the women when I should've been watching the pool. In fact, I was still working at the same pool that I met Marie two years prior. Like Red from *Shawshank Redemption* I could hardly sit still or hold a thought in my head. This was it! Tonight after work, I was going to be moving into my dorm room. I wanted to move in as early as possible, but I knew there was no way I could get off work at the last minute. We were already short-staffed as it was. My creative mind started thinking up a scheme that would allow me to get off work early without looking like a total flake to my employer. Despite the fact that it was my last day for the summer, I had worked for them the two previous summers and didn't want to burn bridges and prevent myself from having such a sweet job next year.

I looked up to the sky as if to pray for rain, but there wasn't a cloud to be seen. Perhaps I could sabotage the chemicals. Yeah, I could say there was a malfunction that made the water unsafe. But, my supervisor was at another pool in the area and he would undoubtedly come by and check things out. As a certified pool operator, I could be fined if they found that the mishap was caused by my negligence, so that wouldn't work. Vomit? Eh, that would only close the pool for an hour. Poop? Hmmm, that would certainly close the pool for at least 24 hours, but how in the world could I pull that one off? I certainly wasn't going to do it myself, and that's not really something you can ask someone to do for you as a favor. I sat there stumped. The wheels in my head were turning, but they weren't really producing a good idea. Then, it hit me. Beyond the pool was a great big field. There were often people out there playing pickup games of football and soccer. It was also a popular spot for the apartment residents to walk their dogs. As in most places, community policy required residents to clean up after their dogs. I looked over at the field only to see Charlie, one of the neighborhood kids, cleaning up after his dog. As he was walking by past the pool to go back to his apartment, I flagged him down and asked him to come over towards the gate.

I had to really think about the proposition I was about to make. It's not often you ask someone to drop their dog's poop into a swimming pool undetected, so you can close up shop early. So, I made my proposition. After laughing to the point of tears, Charlie agreed to do my dirty work, no pun intended, if I gave him $10. Ten bucks was enough to put a tween into a sugar coma the next time the ice cream man came by.

It was as if we were secret agents – like mission impossible. The plan was that he would walk over to the edge of the diving well, away from all of the other patrons. He was going to sit down on the edge of the pool and casually put his feet in the water. Then, when no one was looking he would empty the contents of his grocery bag into the pool, and I would coincidentally walk by a few minutes later and make the discovery. Surprisingly, the plan went off without a hitch. After closing the pool and cleaning up, I clocked out for the last time that summer. I was homeward bound. College, here I come.

Chapter 6: A Snowball's Chance

As weird as it may sound, the hardest thing I had to adjust to my first semester of college was the heat – yes, the heat. You would think that a prestigious state university like the University of Maryland, would be able to provide the incoming freshman with air conditioning, but apparently our tuition wasn't high enough for such luxuries. So, the freshmen were herded into these tall, brick high rise dorms in the middle of August, with no air conditioning. It definitely took some getting use to. It seemed like all the fans in the world couldn't quench the sting of the mid summer sun. Even at night, the heat and humidity were almost unbearable. Sleeping was the worst. I remember taking cold showers right before bed, not drying off, and lying in bed wet with a fan blowing on me, just to get cool enough to fall asleep. Oftentimes, I would wake up sweating in the middle of the night, go take another cold shower, and go back to bed.

That first semester was a blur. I spent most of my time unlearning all of the morals and values my parents spent the first 18 years of my life instilling. My vices became porn, food, and sleep. I was always vulnerable to all three, but without parental supervision, it was easier for me to dig deeper and deeper into a hole.

I was always a good student – much to the dismay of my fellow classmates – even more so because I did it all with less than half the effort that they put forth. I was blessed with an amazing intellect and an outstanding memory. Therefore, the extent of my learning consisted of me going to class, taking notes, and occasionally reviewing those notes. I was never big into studying. I didn't have to be. By writing down what I heard in class, I would soak up the information the first time. This allowed me to put forth minimal effort and still achieve high scholastic marks. I finished high school ranked 17th in a class of 420, and top 5% of the entire county, national merit scholar, yada yada yada. But college was different. I learned that college wasn't necessarily about how smart one was. It was more about how hard one was willing to work to succeed. Let's face it. I was lazy. There's no nice way to sugarcoat the obvious truth. I didn't like working hard, and the fact that I never really had to, made it more difficult for me to start. My secret to success in college was class attendance. If I went to class, I did well. If I didn't, well you get the point.

But this was a new environment for me. I was always popular. I was always social. I was always the life of the party. This made things take a turn for the worse in college, because I didn't have anyone there to reel me back in and keep me focused when I started drifting. I didn't have a curfew. There was no one there making me come back home and go to bed at a certain time. So when my alarm went off at 8 for me to get up and go to class, and I had only been asleep 3 hours, there wasn't anyone to come yank the covers off of me and say, "Boy, get up and go to school!" So I didn't.

I stayed up late, slept in late, and went to class when I felt like it. I wasn't there to learn. I was there to have fun, and every aspect of my life began to reflect it. I didn't notice at first, but I was putting on weight like you wouldn't believe. Everyone talks about the freshman 15, but mine was more like the freshman 50. I've always had a hearty appetite, but I was always active, so I kept a nice balance. I played football in the fall, trained in the winter, played baseball in the spring, and swam in the summer. Throughout high school I weight between 265-285lbs. At 6'1, I was an ideal Guard/Tackle for any high school football program. I even got the attention of some college scouts. I got to eat what I wanted and consistently maintained that weight because I was constantly working out. When I got to college, my lifestyle was sedentary. The only moving I did was walking to class – occasionally. In addition, I got a meal card. All I had to do was go to the cafeteria, get any kind of food I wanted in any quantity I saw fit, and swipe my card. That was it! The combination of gluttonous habits, and inactivity caused me to plump up to 350lbs by the end of my first semester.

During my years in college, I gorged my flesh – in every way possible. I became a gluttonous, fornicating, porn addict. The effects of my lifestyle were taking their toll on my health as well. I was digging a pit deeper and deeper, but my lust for the things of the flesh kept plunging my shovel.

Chapter 7: Look, Mom, No Hands

In the fall of 2001, I decided to try out for the football team at the University of Maryland. My tryout date was actually September 12th, 2001. It was the first year that Ralph Friedgen aka The Fridge took over the program. It had been almost two years since I played in high school, and I was severely out of shape, but I figured I'd give it a go. Much to my surprise, I actually made the team as a walk on. It was one of the best days of my life. I got my own locker and equipment. Everything was so much nicer than the stuff we used in high school. During my extensive physical, the doctors noted that my blood pressure was pretty high. I informed them that I had been on some weight loss medication that caused my pressure to spike for a few hours after taking it. I was told not to take it anymore and to come back in two weeks to get it tested again.

Because I was a walk on and severely out of shape, I wasn't working out with the team – after all, the season had already started. I was on the practice squad and was being groomed to be able to compete the following year. My time was spent in the weight room and at Byrd Stadium running the stairs with the strength and conditioning coach. That was probably the most physically demanding time of my life. It was hard work, but it was worth it. I was dropping weight like crazy. I lost about 15lbs in the first two weeks. When I went back to the doctor to get my blood pressure taken again, it was still dangerously high, despite the fact that I had stopped taking my weight loss medication. I was sent to the lab to get some blood work done. They wanted me to have a lipid panel done so they could officially clear me to play and start working out with the team. When the doctor gave me the form to take to the lab, I asked her if they could do an HIV test while they were testing everything else. She agreed, and made the necessary adjustments on the form. I had never been tested for HIV before. I remember all the commercials on MTV and BET telling you to know you status and such, so I figured now was a better time than ever to have it done. At that point, it had been about three years since I last had sex.

I went to the lab to have my blood drawn on a Thursday. That Friday, I got a voicemail from the doctor saying that the results from my test were in and that she *really* needed to speak with me about the results. I could tell by her tone that she didn't have good news to give me. I called her back immediately, only to get her voicemail. It was late Friday afternoon, and I was sitting by the phone praying to God that she would call me back today. I knew she wouldn't be on campus that weekend, and I don't think I could've lasted that long without knowing what was wrong with me. I waited, and waited, and waited. She didn't call me back. That had to be the longest weekend of my life. I couldn't eat. I couldn't sleep. I sat in my room absolutely miserable. I was in agony.

Finally, I get a call from the doctor on Monday morning, and she asked if I could meet her at the training facility right away. I was on my way running before I hung up the phone. Even if it was bad news – I wanted closure. Not knowing was driving me crazy. When I arrived, she asked me to have a seat. I stared at her intently, trying to see if her face or expression would give anything away. She started speaking slowly and deliberately. I wanted to shout, "Get to the freaking point!" But I would've probably replaced the word "freaking" with something a little less user friendly. She said to me, "I have some very bad news...." There was an agonizing pause as she took a breath. "You have diabetes." I took a deep sigh, and sat there void of expression – completely stoic. She sat in silence as if waiting for me to speak. I took another minute to process the information I had just been given. Slowly, a sense of relief washed over me like a cool summer breeze. Diabetes was a lot better than HIV. My relief, however, was short lived. The doctor told me that my blood pressure and blood sugar were dangerously high and that the medical staff couldn't clear me to play this year. I was given a medical redshirt for the year. I would have to turn in all of my equipment and come back and try out again next year. On my way out, she gave me the name and number of a diabetes specialist and wished me luck. It was a long walk home, most of which I spent crying.

That was a pivotal day in my life. I wish that I could sit here and say that my life changed for the better that morning. In fact, it was quite the opposite. Up to that point I had flown through some turbulent times, but that day caused me to tailspin out of control. My lack of self-control was about to invade every area of my life.

I ended up meeting with the diabetes specialist that the doctor had referred me to. He put me on medication and a very strict, low sugar diet. When he checked my fasting blood sugar, it was upwards of 350. A healthy adult's blood sugar should be close to 100, give or take. When the specialist wrote my prescription for Glucophage, the diabetes medication, he warned me of certain changes that my body would undergo during the process of trying to regulate my blood sugar. He said that my vision would be dramatically impaired for the first ten to fourteen days. He said that I would feel tingling in my hands and feet. He also told me that I could possibly have difficulty achieving an erection. I was less than thrilled about his forecast.

After about a day or so, I realized the severity of my condition. The symptoms occurred exactly the way he described. At first my vision was just a little blurry – as if I had just woken up. After a while, I was completely visually impaired. I couldn't see more than three feet in front of me. I could make out colors and general shapes, but that was about it. I was relieved to discover that if I sat close enough to my computer screen, I could still clearly watch porn. That relief was short-lived when I realized that I wasn't capable of achieving an erection. It was like a cruel joke. Here I was, trapped in my dorm room for almost two weeks – I couldn't watch TV, I could watch porn but couldn't get myself off, and my hands and feet were tingling ALL day as if they were asleep. This was an absolutely miserable existence.

I sat around for two weeks moping and feeling sorry for myself. It was at that time that depression started to take root in my heart. Most of my joy was gone. I wasn't even the same person anymore. Eventually, my vision returned and all of the other symptoms subsided, but I just wasn't happy anymore. I didn't like my life. I didn't like who and what I was becoming, but worst of all, I didn't dislike it all enough to want to change. As much as I hated my behavior and my sins, I had become addicted to the lust that had been conceived and growing within me for so many years.

Chapter 8: Free Fallin'

By the middle of October, I had stopped going to class completely. My days started to run together. I was becoming somewhat nocturnal. I would stay up most of the night and sleep all day. I was gorging my flesh with food and porn. My weight kept increasing, and so did my desire for sex. It had been quite sometime since I had been with a woman, but I became determined to change that. I had made a commitment on November 14, 1998 to wait until I got married to have sex again, but the lust in my heart had developed to the point that I didn't really care anymore. You can't spend hours upon hours watching porn and masturbating and expect your flesh to not want to act out on what you've been feeding it. At that point in my life, I was masturbating at least three times a day. Though I had grown accustomed to studio porn, I was getting really heavy into amateur type stuff. I had developed a taste for the girl-next-door and soccer mom types. I spent a lot of time in adult chat room and adult themed yahoo groups.

One of the things that I noticed about myself is that my sexual appetite was changing. I know now, that it was porn's doing. The thing about internet porn that makes it so appealing is that you can indulge on any fantasy or curiosity that you could possibly imagine. I found myself neck deep in older women seeking young men content. That stemmed from my childhood infatuation with Jack's mom, as I previously mentioned. Remember how I would read literotica stories about the young, handsome pool boy being ravaged by the sultry and seductive housewife? That scenario, and others like it, had become my obsession. It became my focus. I spent countless hours online meeting lonely older women who were interested in meeting young guys. For some odd reason, the idea of being taken advantage of by a cougar sounded appealing to me. It was only a matter of time before the lust that had conceived within me would manifest its fruit.

Sometime thereafter, I met an Argentinean woman online named Maria. She told me that she was 46, but I suspected she was in her early 50's. I was 19 at the time. We spent a few days conversing lustfully online. Eventually our conversations progressed to phone calls. After a while, I knew that meeting up with her was inevitable.

I came up in the Internet generation, and had met my fair share of girls online in the past, but the idea of meeting a *woman* online with the sole purpose of a sexual encounter was both exciting and frightening. Considering she was 46, or so she said, she'd probably been with a *lot* of guys. At 19, I had only been with two girls, so my experience paled in comparison to hers; but for some odd reason, I had a feeling that that was one of the appealing factors for her. She probably felt like she was corrupting a young, innocent boy. Innocence, as I'm told, is quite relative.

We decided to meet up on a Sunday evening. Because I was at school and didn't have my car on campus, she had to come and pick me up. She lived in Bethesda, which wasn't too far away. I sat on the front steps of my building waiting anxiously for her to arrive. After waiting for what felt like ages, I saw a late model Mercedes with tinted windows pull up. The passenger side window came down, and this exotic looking woman said "Hey handsome, you want a ride?" Her voice was so seductive that it gave me chills. I tried to be as cool as possible as I started descending the steps. The coolness expired as I stumbled down the last two steps. I played it off with a goofy grin. Smoooooooooth. I opened the door and hopped in.

If you've ever done any online dating, you're probably quite familiar with the awkwardness that surrounds meeting for the first time. It's about 10x worse when you're meeting people online to just have sex. We made small talk in the car on our way to her house – nothing sexual. I wasn't sure if she was having second thoughts or if I was, but it could've been a combination of the two. I mean, this woman had said some of the raunchiest, sex-inspired things I'd ever heard in my life on the phone and online, but face to face, she seemed a bit timid. Go figure.

We pulled up in the driveway, and I was quite impressed. Her house was *very* nice. When she opened the door, I was enticed by the intoxicating smell of what seemed like an amazing meal that was recently prepared. "I made you some dinner. I hope you're hungry," she said. "In case you couldn't tell by my boyish figure, I'm always hungry," I replied. She escorted me to the dining room where she already had a place setup for me. I sat down while she went into the kitchen. She made me an enormous plate of chicken, rice and beans and sat it down right in front of me. She didn't eat, which seemed odd to me. She just sat there watching me intently as I ate. We made casual conversation, but things felt a little awkward. After I finished eating, she cleared my plate from the table and casually asked me if I wanted to "see" her bedroom. I figured that was code for: are you ready to do what I brought you over to do. I obliged and followed her up to her room.

Her bedroom was just as nice as the rest of the house. The first thing I noticed was a small digital video camera sitting on the dresser. I picked it up and asked her what she had in mind. "The only thing more exciting than an awesome sexual encounter is being able to watch all of the naughty details over and over again," she said. At the time, I was all about having sex, but the idea of having a recording of my sexual misconduct floating around for the rest of my life was less than appealing to me. "Maybe next time," I said, hoping that she would take the hint. It didn't seem to bother her, which was a huge relief for me.

As things progressed, I realized that I was in over my head. I felt like a rookie quarterback in the NFL getting his first game time action in the Super Bowl with my team down by six and two minutes left in the game. The pressure was too much to bear. My less than stellar performance was interrupted by a phone call. She answered in Spanish. After a very brief conversation, she hung up the phone quickly and told me that I had to leave because her husband and her mother-in-law were on the way over. Husband?? That was news to me. So, not only was I a fornicator, I was an adulterer as well. Great.

She drove me back to my dorm, and I made the walk of shame. That evening I felt like something died inside of me. That event caused a chain reaction in my life. Despite hating myself for it, those kinds of encounters started to come regularly though not with the same people. My college years were spent drinking, watching porn, and fornicating.

I found myself in a position many Christians find themselves. You know enough about God to not be able to fully enjoy your sin, yet you don't know enough about God to use his Word and His principles to be able to experience true and complete deliverance from it. Such was my life for many years.

The next few years of my life were spent in a spiritual wilderness. I felt as if God wasn't my father anymore. Rather, he was a distant relative that I barely remember who despite my indifference still loved me enough to send me a card on my birthday, just to let me know He still cared. But then again, that's how God is. Even when we ignore Him, even when we leave Him to go do our own thing, even when we take Him for granted, He still loves us. My wife is proof. I didn't deserve a woman like her, but one day....she showed up.

Chapter 9: A Blessing in the Storm

I met Jess in October of 2006. The story of how we met isn't all that exciting. She likes to tell people that we met through a mutual friend named Craig, but the complete truth is that we met on Craigslist. That's right – a free internet classified ad. Who would've thought you could meet your spouse there? I certainly didn't. I'm sure she didn't either. But so it was.

She had a post up saying that she was looking for a nice Christian guy, that she wanted to date with purpose, and that she wasn't giving in to sexual advances until she was married. I was impressed by her candor and straight talk. Her sweet spirit and Christian values appealed to my better side, and her appearance appealed to everything else. We started by exchanging e-mails, then phone calls. A few days later we agreed to meet. We decided to meet at the Mall in Columbia, which was rather close to my house.

It's funny how people can forget important information, but never forget the small details that makeup a particular moment. I remember parking on the top level of the parking garage and taking the elevator down. As soon as the doors closed, I knew I had made a mistake. I should've taken the stairs, or climbed over the railing and jumped to the ground floor. This thing definitely wasn't in as big of a hurry as I was. We had spoken shortly before, so I knew she was on the ground floor by the elevator waiting for me. Still, this thing was taking it's sweet old time. I stared up at the numbers as if waiting for the last number to appear on a million dollar bingo card. Life was in slooooooow motion. 3..........2.............1......... As the doors opened, I beheld a beauty that I had never seen to that point in my life and haven't seen in another woman since. There she was – gorgeous, shapely, and TALL. My goodness; she was six feet. I only had her beat by an inch. She had flawless skin, a radiant smile, brown hair, and green eyes that looked like a pair of sparkling emeralds. I was captivated. I am still captivated.

We exchanged pleasantries. Then, she held my hand as we walked towards to mall. I was in heaven. She smelled amazing. All of my carnal senses were going bonkers, but the only thing I could feel was my heart thumping in my throat. We walked towards the food court to sit down and talk. After a few minutes, I realized that I had scored a total package. To go along with that amazing exterior, she had a great personality, a wealth of wisdom, and a witty intellect.

I knew at that moment that I wanted to forsake all others and pursue her. Surprisingly, I told her that. Even more surprisingly, she felt the same way. At that moment our journey began. Now, I know what you're thinking. You're thinking, "I don't believe in that love at first sight crap." Well, neither do I. But I do know a good thing when I see it. And I knew right then that I didn't want to look any further. I wanted to explore things with her. Turns out, I've got excellent judgment.

Our relationship had an unusually long "honeymoon" phase. You know that phase where the other person is *perfect*? Well, I realize now that the phase was prolonged because we both did a pretty good job of hiding our flaws and reality in general from each other. I kept my addiction secret from her, and she masked the things she struggled with from me. For a while, the relationship was emotionally superficial. We both made each other *feel* good, but there was no substance to our relationship because both of us were afraid to expose our true selves to the other person.

I'm not exactly sure how it came up, but at some point, a few months later, I told her about my struggles with porn. Of course, I left out all of the graphic details and tried to guise it in an "all guys do it" kind of light. I mean, why not? I had talked to previous girlfriends about it, and all of them took the "boys will be boys" approach and left me alone about it. Jess was different. Instead of letting me slide and not holding me accountable, she started asking me rather probing questions. I did not like that at all. Having dealt with the issue for most of my life, I found solace and comfort in keeping my issues secret. I had never truly been exposed to anyone other than God. Jess was the first person to make serious efforts to seek the truth in me. Though I know now that it was a good thing for me, I hated it at the time. I felt so violated and exposed.

I didn't realize that my actions and words could cause so much pain. Being the self-centered, self-concerned, self-worshipping, self-pleasing porn addict that I was, the concept of considering other people was rather foreign to me. I didn't understand why my looking at porn bothered her so much, and she didn't understand why I didn't understand. It was like we were going in circles – lost in the wilderness, walking around the same mountain over and over again.

I prayed about it. I didn't feel like God had really given me an answer. I asked for forgiveness, but I still felt the same. I vowed to myself and to Jess that I was done with porn. That lasted about three months. I fell off the wagon. Then the wagon backed up and ran over me. Then the wagon driver climbed down and shot me a couple times. Then, well, you get the point. We did that song and dance for over a year. I would mess up, then she would be upset, and then I'd promise not to do it again - again, around the same mountain. After a while she had had enough. She told me that if I looked at porn one more time, I was choosing porn over her and that she would end the relationship. That was some serious motivation. We had recently been engaged, we were planning a wedding, and the idea of losing her because of an out-of-control addiction and having to explain that to all my friends and family who were expecting a wedding was frightening. I was determined to change....for a while, that is until my flesh started talking to me again. Anyone who has ever had a sexual compulsion, or any kind of compulsive addiction for that matter, can attest to the fact that when your flesh and those desires start talking to you, most people throw logic and sound judgment out the window. Why else would men risk their marriages, their families, their financial future, their health, and ultimately their lives to temporarily satisfy these cravings?

I believed the Enemy's lie. He told me that I couldn't change. He told me that no one else understood, least of all my fiancée. He told me that porn was my only option at this point and that it would bridge the gap between a single, sexless lifestyle to the sexual utopia called marriage (most of the married guys are probably scratching their heads because they didn't get the memo about marriage being a sexual utopia). Regardless of how absurd those lies sound right now, I believed them at the time. I believed them for most of my life

Since I didn't think I could fix the problem, I stopped being honest with her about it. I built my kingdom with lies. Deception and secrecy were my brick and mortar. My perverted sense of logic said that if I couldn't stop, at least I could try to get her off my back about it by not being honest. Once we got married and could have sex, the issue would work itself out, so why make a big stink about it now? The Enemy's lies had become my mission statements. The problem is I later found out that lying to her was doing more damage than just confessing. Eventually, I was caught. I was always caught. You would think I would learn after the first time, but I was determined to learn the hard way over and over again. This is s public service announcement: if you lie, you will eventually be exposed. The Bible is very clear about that. Everything done in secret will be exposed to the light. This is *especially* true if the person you're lying to is born again, filled with the spirit, and in constant communion with Holy Spirit. The Bible says that it is Holy Spirit's job to lead and guide us into all truth. I personally believe that the feminine spirit is dramatically more sensitive to Holy Spirit than the masculine spirit. Some people call it women's intuition. I think that's why God intended for them to help us, because often times we're too busy or too focused to see or hear what God wants us to do, so He'll let us know through our wives. It's a wonderful thing if you're a man who listens to your wife. It's an excellent tool to have when you're walking in God's best in your relationship and the two of you are unified. It's a nightmare if you're the type of guy who doesn't respect or honor her thoughts and opinions, or when you're lying to her and trying to keep things hidden.

They say that the definition of insanity is doing the same thing over and over again expecting different results. I guess if that's true then I definitely "flew over the cuckoo's nest." I had such pride that I always thought that I was smart enough to be able to get away with it. That kingdom of lies that I was building, the one that I thought was my solace, my sanctuary – well it turned out that I was building my own prison. I was so afraid of being exposed that I became painfully paranoid. I thought every question was an accusation. It's funny how that works, really. I was the one who had broken her trust so many times, and after all that, I started becoming suspicious and not trusting her.

Chapter 10: Rock Bottom

Feels like your world is caving in
And I cry failing to understand, I wish I can
It's alright if you're missing Him
In His eyes you can live again, free within

Time after time, I walk the fine line
Something keeps bringing me back
And time after time, I'm going in blind
I don't know which way I need to go
P.O.D – Going In Blind

A lot of addiction specialists agree that a person has to hit rock bottom before he is going to have any desire or motivation to want to change. I would agree with that statement if you would first concede the fact that the person is a fool. I would also agree on the condition that not everyone's rock bottom is the same, and what may be the lowest point for one would be an ideal destination compared to another's situation. I've read stories about other peoples' descent to their rock bottom. I read of men whose flesh was so out of control due to years and years of feeding it porn that they went out and spent thousands of dollars on prostitutes, broke their marriage vows, and got an STD that they brought home and shared with their wives. I've also heard of pastors who let their flesh get out of control and acted on their unnatural desires with another man, exposing their lives, their ministries, and the entire Christian community to the media backlash and scrutiny that comes along with such behavior. Granted, my rock bottom was nowhere near *Jerry Springer* material the way the previous examples were. It was, however, enough to shake the foundations of my life, and it did force me to the defining moment in my life – a proverbial fork in the road.

June 20, 2008: There are certain days, moments, and periods of time that stand out in your life as significant. I remember that it was a Friday. I was finishing up a hard day's work and looking forward to a weekend that I knew wouldn't be long enough. At 4:30 I was wrapping up my day when my manager called me into the conference room. When I got there, there was another manager sitting at the table. I knew this wouldn't be good. I sat down cautiously, wondering what was about to transpire. My manager wasted no time in getting to the point. He told me that it just wasn't working out, and that today would be my last day with the company. He said that they were paying me six weeks of severance, and that he wished me all the best. Just like that. I was done. I had been with the company for over six months, and in the blink of an eye my future there was no more. Even worse was the fact that he really wouldn't give me a straight answer as to why. He just kept saying that it wasn't working out, and it wasn't the best fit. The best fit? It took you six months to realize it wasn't the best fit? Maybe that's your failure as a manager. I came closer to reaching across the table and punching him in his smug little face than I ever had in the six months I worked there. But common sense got the better of me. The only thing worse than being unemployed 98 days before you're supposed to be getting married is being unemployed and in jail. I returned to my desk, packed my things, and did the walk of shame out to the parking lot. They weren't even nice enough to give me a box, so I had all of my personal belongings in my arms. I was struggling to make it out to the car without dropping anything when my manager came running out after me. Perhaps he was going to apologize. Maybe he was going to offer me some words of advice or wisdom. "Oh yeah, I need your keys to the building," he said. Maybe not.

When I got in the car, things really started to sink in. To be honest, I wasn't mad. I hated that job to begin with, it was 32 miles away from my house in a time when gas prices were upwards of $4.00 a gallon, and my manager was a self-righteous brat. Seriously, I was not upset about the job. I was upset about having to explain the situation to my bride-to-be. We were in the process of pre-marital counseling and in that process I learned that one of Jess' most important emotional needs was financial security. I knew that all too well, hence my apprehension about the whole situation.

Jess was at the hospital because her sister gave birth to a beautiful baby boy named Thomas the day before. It was planned ahead of time that I would visit the hospital that day after work to spend time with the family.

Pause. It's awesome watching Thomas grow up. He's like a living mile marker for me. The last time I looked at porn was the day he was born. I watched him grow. I watched him learn to walk and talk. I watched him turn into this handsome little boy. And every time I see him, I am reminded of the life I left behind. *Play*

I called Jess like I normally did as I left work. I told her what had just happened. At first she thought I was joking. When she finally realized that I was being serious, the playful banter stopped. I could hear the concern in her words as her voice trembled. I knew that it took all the strength she had not to break down and cry right there. But she had to maintain. She had to stay strong. We couldn't let her parents know.....just yet. Her parents were rather old fashioned....and by old fashioned I mean that they had issues with their white daughter being with a black man. In the beginning of our relationship it was pretty rough. There were a lot of awkward silences. As time passed and they got to know me, they opened up a lot more. I felt that all the progress we had made would be in jeopardy due to my newly acquired unemployment. I could hear all of the lazy, non-working black guy dating the I'm-more-than-willing-to-support-you-if-I-have-to white girl stereotypes replaying themselves in my head.

That blow was a strain on our relationship. She was afraid. I was afraid. What was I to do? It's much easier to comfort someone and tell them it's going to be okay when you truly believe it. But what happens when you question it yourself? How do you convince someone to believe something that you're not even sure you believe in? There is an answer to every question. I was about to learn the answer to mine.

The next day was a lazy Saturday. I pretty much sat around playing Halo 3 all day as if the answers to my problems could be found in a Slayer match at The Narrows. Sadly, no answers could be found there. But that day, God – my creator, was about to send me a message loud and clear.

I had gotten ready for church that Saturday evening and was waiting for Jess to arrive at my house. While I was waiting, I called one of the guys I worked with to see if he knew anything more about my unceremonious firing. Jess came in shortly after while I was still on the phone with Ryan. She asked me to see the laptop so she could check movie times. We usually went out to dinner and to a movie on Saturday nights after church. I panicked for a second, wondering if I had cleared the history since the last time I fed my flesh its regular filth. Remembering that I hadn't gotten myself off since the day prior, I was sure I had cleared the history and was in the clear. I was wrong. While I was still on the phone, Jess spun the laptop around so I could see it, exposing the trail of porn sites logged in the computer's history. I could see the hurt and pain on her face as the tears began to well up. "Are you still looking at porn? Yes or No?" she demanded. Meanwhile, I'm still on the phone with Ryan, but I knew he could sense something was wrong. "Hey Ryan, I gotta go," I said. Again, she demanded, "Yes or No?" My mind was racing, I was trying to conjure up a lie, but I was drawing a blank. I knew I got caught with my pants down, literally. "Yes," I reluctantly admitted. Before I could fully get the words out of my mouth, she had spun around and stormed out of the room, violently slamming the door behind her. I sat there in disbelief for a moment. I felt so exposed, so ashamed. I wanted to crawl into a ditch somewhere and die. I was expecting to hear her car speeding away, but instead I heard Jess making her way back to my room. She opened the door again and demanded answers. I didn't feel much like talking. I didn't know what to say. Besides, I had no credibility with her at the moment, so I doubted anything I said would've been believed.

As if it couldn't get any worse, she called my mom and told her to change the laptop password ASAP because I had been looking at porn....on her work laptop. So, not only was my secret exposed to Jessica, but now my parents knew about it as well. My den of lies and secrecy was imploding all around me, and Jess was holding the dynamite.

To this day, that was the lowest point in my life. I felt lower than a bow-legged caterpillar. I lost my job, and I felt like I was about to lose my Jess. I had reached my rock bottom. There wasn't a place any lower that I could've sunk. My head hurt. My heart hurt. Everything hurt. But what I didn't know at the time was that my greatest triumph was going to arise from the ashes of my greatest defeat. In the midst of the storm I heard the Lord speak to me. There have been a few times in my life where I knew that I heard God. Mostly I heard from Holy Spirit. For me He speaks in that gentle, you-need-to-be-paying-attention-to-hear-me voice – that subtle urging or prodding that feels like a good idea that came out of nowhere. That's how I normally heard from God. But this time, this time was different. There was nothing subtle or gentle about it. I distinctly heard the Lord ask me, "Do I have your attention now?"

I believe the question was more rhetorical than anything, because the answer was painfully obvious. I didn't have much of a choice at that point. I had tried for so long to do things my own way, and I kept falling flat on my face. I spent my life like the Israelites in Exodus wandering around the same mountain out in the wilderness, and God invaded my little world to show me the way out. This was my chance to listen. This was my chance to show others the way. This was my calling.

Chapter 11: The Road Less Traveled

I spent the next few days in God's presence. I asked forgiveness of my sins, but more importantly I repented and made a commitment to turn from them for good. I didn't quite know how I was going to do it, but I knew it needed to be done. I prayed earnestly and relied on God to show me the way. I remember feeling the Spirit of the Lord speak to me. It was almost like Morpheus talking to Neo. "I can only show you the door, but you have to walk through it."

I discovered an intimacy with my Father that I didn't know existed. This wasn't like before. This wasn't lip service. This was true and unadulterated repentance. I cried out to God, and he listened. He had broken me, but he also comforted me during the healing process. That's why He's the Good Shepherd. There's something really profound and prophetic in calling God our Shepherd. David said in the 23rd Psalm, "thy rod and thy staff they comfort me." The rod is for correction, but the staff is for support. The two go hand in hand. It's a process that God had to take me through. When a shepherd loses a wandering sheep, he goes after it. When a sheep continues to wander after that point, the shepherd will break the sheep's legs so it cannot wander anymore. Have you ever seen a picture or a painting of a shepherd carrying a sheep draped across his neck and shoulders? Well now you know why. That's part of the training process. During that process the sheep has to learn to be fully dependent on its shepherd because with a few broken legs, it can't really do anything on its own. It has to learn dependence, much like we need to learn dependence. We spend most of our lives trying to gain our independence. Whether it's taking our first steps, going to play beyond the restrictive border of our fenced yard, getting our driver's license, or even moving out of our parents' house. Independence is what we crave, but God, our Father, wants to teach us complete and total dependence. That's the starting point. That's our foundation.

Our God is a jealous God. He wants to know that He is your first priority, and He despises anything that comes between you and Him. In my personal situation, it was my flesh. I had spent 16 years of my life indulging my flesh to the point where it became my god. My constant service was a form of worship, and God was jealous. He didn't have my affections the way He desired, and it took something drastic for Him to get my attention.

Despite growing up in a Christian family and being able to quote enough scripture to make an avid Bible thumper proud, I was missing a key ingredient – my heart. Up to this point in my life I never really wanted to change. My heart was tainted.

From a spiritual standpoint, our heart refers to our soul. It's our thought process. Our hearts and minds are interchangeable, synonymous. Just as God is a triune being, we are triune beings. During the story of creation when God said, "Let us make man in our image and in our likeness," He was not talking about our physical bodies. God is a spirit. He doesn't have a physical body. Rather, He was referring to our complete makeup, as well as our temperament and emotions. Just as God is a spirit, we too are spirits. We were fashioned to be just like Him. If you look at all the wonders of the universe, you can't help but be amazed by the creativity and sheer awesomeness of God. Look at how many species of animals there are, or look at all of the different varieties of subspecies within a single species. God has unmatched creativity, but when it came to creating mankind – his greatest creation – He did not need His creativity. He could simply look into a mirror and derive the blueprint for creating us.

Consider this: we are a spirit, we have a soul, and we live in a body. Throughout our lives our spirit and our flesh will constantly war over our soul (heart). God is in tune with our spirits, while Satan manipulates and entices our flesh. Whichever is stronger will dominate the tug-of-war for our soul and our overall attention. During most of my life, I spent far more time feeding my flesh and starving my spirit. Because of that behavior, I had gotten to the point where my flesh was out of control. I couldn't say no.

> *Do not be deceived, God is not mocked: for whatever a man sows, that he will also reap. For he who sows to his flesh, will of the flesh reap corruption, but he who sows to the Spirit will of the Spirit reap everlasting life.*
> Galatians 6:7-8

Chapter 12: Redemption

Long is the way, and hard, that out of hell leads up to light.
Paradise Lost – John Milton

The week that followed was a pivotal time for me. There are certain moments in people's lives that have the ability to determine where the rest of their lives are going to go. At the fork in the road, which path will you choose? I had two options in front of me: I could temporarily learn my lesson, fake a life-altering experience, and eventually continue following the path I had been following up to that point; or I could truly and genuinely receive my deliverance, choose to walk in it, and step out in faith and follow God in a new direction. For the first time in my life, I chose to be a man and take the more difficult road. I chose the latter. I followed God into the great unknown. Much like the time when God told Abram to pack up his things, leave his father's house, and follow Him to a place He would lead to. I too had no idea where the Lord was taking me.

Some people feel that it's easier to trust God when things are going right. I, on the other hand, believe the opposite is true for me. I've found that challenges prove character. In my life, when things were going well I subconsciously thought that I could do things on my own and didn't need God's help. Perhaps my outlook is the reason God allowed things to happen the way they did. God knew that it would take something dramatic to get my attention. I believe that's the great thing about God. He's personally involved in every believer's life to the point where He knows exactly how to deal with each and every one of us, right down to our own specific circumstances.

I found myself in a position where I had to trust God. I didn't have a job. My relationship with my fiancée was critically wounded, and I was trying to overcome an addiction that had plagued me for all of my adult life. This was a challenging time, but for the first time in my life I *knew* I wasn't going at it alone. I learned that my relationship with God was not about feelings. I learned how to trust God, even when I couldn't feel His presence. I learned to have faith in Him, even when the situation looked bad. I learned how to walk with God. Many Christians don't know how to walk with God. There's a huge difference between being saved and having a personal relationship with Him. I knew God in the sense that I believed He was God and sent His son to die for my sins. It wasn't a question of my salvation. The question was all about my walk. Up to that point I failed to realize the importance of a personal relationship with Him, and never truly developed one.

Jessica also noticed the change in my life. She knew me better than anyone in the world, and she knew that the transformation was genuine. Though I had hurt her, lied to her, and repeatedly abused the trust she had in me, she found it in her heart to forgive me and continue to move forward in our relationship. And for that, I am truly grateful.

Because I grew up in a Christian home and had a strong knowledge of the scriptures, my faith grew exponentially as I began to put into practice the Word that I had hidden deep within my Spirit. The entire time I was in bondage to sin, specifically porn and lust, I had all of the tools I needed to succeed. I just didn't know how to tap into those abilities.

I didn't stay unemployed long. In fact, I started getting paychecks from my new job while I was still collecting severance from my old one. God is good. At my new job I was making a lot more money while working less hours, and to really sweeten the deal, the office was located about four miles from my house. I was definitely pleased with the job opportunity. Jess was ecstatic. We continued to spend the next couple months finishing up the wedding plans and completing our pre-marital counseling curriculum. We were married on September 26, 2008 – which will forever be the happiest day of my life.

Act II: Side Effects May Include….

Chapter 13: Read the Fine Print

I am my own affliction
I am my own disease
There ain't no drug that they could sell
No, there ain't no drug to make me well
There ain't no drug
There ain't no drug
There ain't no drug
It's not enough
The sickness is myself.
Switchfoot – Mess of Me

     I'm going to get back to my story eventually and go through the steps I took to receive my deliverance, but first I want to lay the foundation and show you the dangers of pornography. I personally didn't fully appreciate being delivered from an addiction to lust and porn until I really understood what it was doing to me. Pornography is like a nuclear bomb. With a nuclear weapon you have devastating immediate effects like vaporization – where a concentrated area is just annihilated, destroyed. After vaporization, you have to deal with nuclear radiation. Though more subtle and cunning than vaporization, radiation is just as dangerous. Porn works the same way. There are some things that you will see and notice immediately – which you will immediately attribute to porn consumption – while there are some other things that will take some time to develop and germinate after the lust has been conceived in your heart, but when they show up they will be equally as dangerous. Without direction or instruction it's difficult for one to link the connection between those particular behaviors and porn. Most, if not all, of these behaviors and side effects are interconnected with each other. They are all related because they all stem from the same source. The good news is that if you can get to the root, it's easy to kill the branches. Cut off the head, and everything else dies.

Chapter 14: Perversion

One of the things Satan is famous for is taking something beautiful that God has created and twisting it into something vile and unholy. Sex is obviously his favorite target. God created sex to be an invaluable gift to married couples. In the context of a loving marriage, sex is for procreation as well as recreation. With pornography, the enemy has taken one of God's greatest creations and defiled it. Instead of sex being shared between a husband and a wife, it's now shared with everyone: men, women, children, animals, and even oneself. Though you can't blame porn for the conception of these immoral practices since all of these have been around long before porn in the modern era, you can fault porn for dramatically spreading the practices and behaviors. If these behaviors were like a small brush fire in an unsuspecting California forest, then porn is the dry climate, strong winds, and gasoline that spread something small and manageable into a disaster of epidemic proportions. Porn is a multi-billion dollar industry. Next year, pornography will generate more revenue than the NFL, NBA and MLB combined....several times over. The sad thing is that those statistics only include legal, traceable revenue generated by porn sales. It doesn't include revenue generated by illegal forms of porn, prostitution, exotic dancers, international sex slaves, and many other forms of profitable deviant behavior.

To say that sex sells is an understatement of almost grossly negligent proportions. It's like saying that the best use of the Bible is for its historical content. You cannot turn on the TV without seeing some scantly clad dame prancing around selling something. What in the world do half-clothed women have to do with beer? Nothing. But beer executives know that if some chick is almost naked, most men are going to be paying attention which in turn will increase the likelihood of them buying the product. And that's pretty sad.

An indulgence in pornography also leads to perversion because it has a way of desensitizing us. I remember when I was young, before I had been introduced to pornography, seeing a woman in her underwear via a Sears catalog was enough to get me physically aroused. I remember sitting in my room watching the Spice channel, being completely and totally turned on because a woman was slowly dancing around naked....and I was watching it on a scrambled television. Just the thought of catching a glimpse of boob was enough excitement for me to get myself off. Over the years, the indulgence continued to desensitize.

After a while, softcore porn was no longer enough. The racy scenes from HBO and Skin-O-Max (Cinemax) weren't enough to fully arouse me. I needed to see more. I needed to see penetration. I needed hardcore porn. After taking that next step I was satisfied, but only temporarily. Eventually my flesh would require more. Soon, hardcore wasn't enough. I needed to see anal. After that I started being intrigued and interested in more weird and rather unconventional types of porn. I found myself seeking videos of midgets, fat women, old women, and everything in between. I even watched bisexual porn, gay porn, pre and post-op transexual porn. It got to the point where I was a product of a debased mind as described in the first chapter of Romans. Virtually nothing was off limits as far as my viewing pleasure was concerned. Once that snowball started rolling down hill, it was only a matter of time before I lost complete and total control of it. Remember, lust can **never** be quenched.

I used to get lot of porn from P2P file sharing programs. Sometimes if I found a user with a fast connection, I would download their entire porn collection – not knowing what I'd find. I used to do this at night so that every morning was like Christmas as I'd get to sort through gigs and gigs of porn that downloaded as I slept.

It was then that I had my first and only experience with child pornography. One of the users I downloaded from had a large collection of homemade videos that showed adults, both male and female, being sexually intimate with underage children. Some of them were tweens, and some of the children were as young as 2 or 3. It was absolutely disgusting, but I couldn't look away. It was like witnessing a gruesome car accident, my eyes couldn't believe what they were seeing and my mind couldn't comprehend what was actually happening. I was in utter disbelief. I felt sorry for the kids. I knew they probably had a life full of pain and poor choices ahead of them due to their abuse. They reminded me of myself. I couldn't help but wonder what would possess an adult to do that to a child, but deep, deep down, I knew. I'd bet you my life it probably started with their own abuse, followed by large amounts of porn consumption that led to acting out like that.

I read an article written by Donald L. Hilton, Jr. called *How Pornography Drugs & Changes Your Brain.* It was one of the most comprehensive explanations addressing the addictive nature of porn from a scientific approach that I've ever read. After reading it, I'm sure you will agree.

While some have avoided using the term "addiction" in the context of natural compulsions such as uncontrolled sexuality, overeating, or gambling, let us consider current scientific evidence regarding the brain and addiction.

This article will seek to answer two questions: (1) Biologically, is the brain affected by pornography and other sexual addictions? (2) If so, and if such addictions are widespread, can they have a societal effect as well?

The Story of the Gypsy Moth

Let's begin with a seeming digression. In 1869 the gypsy moth was brought to America to attempt to jumpstart a silk industry. Rarely have good intentions gone so wrong, as the unforeseen appetite of the moth for deciduous trees such as oaks, maples, and elms has devastated forests for 150 years. Numerous attempts were made to destroy this pest, but a major breakthrough came in the 1960s, when scientists noted that the male gypsy moth finds a female to mate with by following her scent. This scent is called a pheromone, and is extremely attractive to the male.

In 1971 a paper was published in the journal *Nature* that described how pheromones were used to prevent the moths from mating. The scientists mass-produced the pheromone and permeated the moths' environment with it. This unnaturally strong scent overpowered the females' normal ability to attract the male, and the confused males were unable to find females. A follow-up paper described how population control of the moths was achieved by "preventing male gypsy moths from finding mates."

The gypsy moth was the first insect to be controlled by the use of pheromones, which work by two methods. One is called the confusion method. An airplane scatters an environmentally insignificant number of very small plastic pellets imbedded with the scent of the pheromone. Then, as science journalist Anna Salleh describes it, "The male either becomes confused and doesn't know which direction to turn for the female, or he becomes desensitized to the lower levels of pheromones naturally given out by the female and has no incentive to mate with her."

The other method is called the trapping method: Pheromone-infused traps are set, from which moths cannot escape; a male moth enters looking for a female, only to find a fatal substitute.

Two Fallacies

What does this have to do with pornography? Pornography is a visual pheromone, a powerful, $100 billion per year brain drug that is changing human sexuality by "inhibiting orientation" and "disrupting pre-mating communication between the sexes by permeating the atmosphere," especially through the internet. I believe we are currently struggling in the war against pornography because many continue to believe two key fallacies:

Fallacy No. 1: Pornography is not a drug.
Fallacy No. 2: Pornography is therefore not a real addiction.

As an illustration of Fallacy No. 1, consider the following statement by a Wall Street executive whose mainstream company discreetly profits from pornography: "I'm not a weirdo or a pervert, it's not my deal. I've got kids and a family. But if I can see as an underwriter going out and making bucks on people being weird, hey, dollars are dollars. I'm not selling drugs. It's Wall Street."

Now consider both fallacies as elucidated in the following statement by an executive in the pornography industry:

[T]he fact [is] that "drugs, booze and cigarettes" are all physical, chemical agents that are ingested and can indeed have measurable, harmful, addictive effects. The mere viewing of any type of subject matter hardly falls into this category and, in fact, belittles the very real battles that addicts face over drugs, booze and cigarettes—all of which can be lethal. No one ever died from looking at porn. While some compulsive types can be "addicted" to anything, such as watching a favorite television show, eating ice cream or going to the gym, nobody suggests that ice cream is akin to crack cocaine [remember that statement] and should be regulated to protect . . . people from themselves—instead, these compulsive actions are rightfully viewed by society as personality defects in the individual. . . .

Here I will review some of the science he refers to, and also discuss whether pornography is a "physical, chemical" agent, i.e., "a drug," and also consider the latest research on natural brain rewards in deciding whether it is a true brain addiction.

Adrenaline Grass

First, I would like to share an experience our family had a few years ago on a safari in Africa. While on a game drive along the Zambezi River, our ranger commented on the adrenaline grass growing along the banks. I asked him why he used the word "adrenaline," and he began to drive slowly through the grass. Abruptly, he stopped the vehicle and said, "There! Do you see it?"
"See what?" I asked. He drove closer, and this also changed the angle of the light.

Then I understood. A lion was hiding in the grass watching the river, just waiting for some "fast food" to come and get a drink.

We were sitting in an open-air Land Rover with no doors and no windows. I then understood why it was called adrenaline grass, as I felt my heart pound. My cerebral cortex saw and defined the danger, which registered in the autonomic, or automatic, part of my nervous system. The brain, which is a very efficient pharmaceutical lab, produced the chemical adrenaline, causing my heart to pound and race in preparation for survival. I was ready to run if needed (not that it would have done any good with the lion).

We were told that if we stayed in our seats and remained still, the lion would look at the Land Rover as a whole and not see us as individuals. Fortunately this was the case for us.

A Drug Is a Drug

Interestingly, adrenaline, also called epinephrine, is a drug we physicians use in surgery and in emergencies to start a patient's heart again when it beats too slow, or even stops. So here is the question: Is epinephrine not a drug if the brain makes it (causing the heart to pound and race), yet is a drug if the same epinephrine is given by a physician?

Or consider dopamine. This chemical is a close cousin to epinephrine, both of which are excitatory neurotransmitters that tell the brain to Go! Dopamine is important in the parts of our brain that allow us to move, and when the dopamine-producing parts of the brain are damaged, Parkinson's disease results. To treat Parkinson's, physicians prescribe dopamine as a drug, and it helps the patient move again. So is dopamine a drug only if the pharmaceutical lab makes it, and not if the brain makes the same chemical for the same purpose?

Of course, both are drugs in every sense of the word, regardless of where they are produced. Pertinent to our subject, it happens that both of these brain drugs are very important in human sexuality—and in pornography and sexual addiction. Dopamine, in addition to its role in movement, is an integral neurotransmitter, or brain drug, in the pleasure/reward system in the brain.

Disruption of Dopamine

Let's review some of the important components of the reward system of the brain. On the outside is the cerebral cortex, a layer of nerve cells that carry conscious, volitional thought. In the front, over the eyes, are the frontal lobes. These areas are important in judgment, and, if the brain were a car, the frontal lobes would be the brakes. These lobes have important connections to the pleasure pathways, so pleasure can be controlled.

In the center of the brain is the nucleus accumbens. This almond-sized area is a key pleasure reward center, and when activated by dopamine and other neurotransmitters, it causes us to value and desire pleasure rewards. Dopamine is essential for humans to desire and value appropriate pleasure in life. Without it, we would not be as incentivized to eat, procreate, or even to try to win a game.

It's the overuse of the dopamine reward system that causes addiction. When the pathways are used compulsively, a downgrading occurs that actually decreases the amount of dopamine in the pleasure areas available for use, and the dopamine cells themselves start to atrophy, or shrink. The reward cells in the nucleus accumbens are now starved for dopamine and exist in a state of dopamine craving, as a downgrading of dopamine receptors on the pleasure cells occurs as well. This resetting of the "pleasure thermostat" produces a "new normal." In this addictive state, the person must act out in addiction to boost the dopamine to levels sufficient just to feel normal.

As the desensitization of the reward circuits continues, stronger and stronger stimuli are required to boost the dopamine. In the case of narcotic addiction, the addicted person must increase the amount of the drug to get the same high. In pornography addiction, progressively more shocking images are required to stimulate the person.

Frontal Lobe Damage

As a feedback of sorts, the frontal lobes also atrophy, or shrink. Think of it as a "wearing out of the brake pads." This physical and functional decline in the judgment center of the brain causes the person to become impaired in his ability to process the consequences of acting out in addiction. Addiction scientists have called this condition hypofrontality, and have noted a similarity in the behavior of addicted persons to the behavior of patients with frontal brain damage.

Neurosurgeons frequently treat people with frontal lobe damage. In a car crash, for instance, the driver's brain will often decelerate into the back of his forehead inside his skull, bruising the frontal lobes. Patients with frontal lobe damage exhibit a constellation of behaviors we call frontal lobe syndrome. First, these patients are impulsive, in that they thoughtlessly engage in activities with little regard to the consequences. Second, they are compulsive; they become fixated or focused on certain objects or behaviors, and have to have them, no matter what. Third, they become emotionally labile, and have sudden and unpredictable mood swings. Fourth, they exhibit impaired judgment.

So cortical hypofrontality, or shrinkage of the frontal lobes, causes these four behaviors, and they can result from a car wreck or from addiction.

A study on cocaine addiction published in 2002 shows volume loss, or shrinkage, in several areas of the brain, particularly the frontal control areas. A study from 2004 shows very similar results for methamphetamine. But we expect drugs to damage the brain, so these studies don't really surprise us.

Consider, though, a natural addiction, such as overeating leading to obesity. You might be surprised to learn that a study published in 2006 showed shrinkage in the frontal lobes in obesity very similar to that found in the cocaine and methamphetamine studies. And a study published in 2007 of persons exhibiting severe sexual addiction produced almost identical results to the cocaine, methamphetamine, and obesity studies. (Encouragingly, two studies, one on drug addiction [methamphetamine] and one on natural addiction [obesity] also show a return to more normal frontal lobe volumes with time in recovery.)

So we have four studies, two drug and two natural addiction studies, all done in different academic institutions by different research teams, and published over a five-year period in four different peer-reviewed scientific journals. And all four studies show that addictions physically affect the frontal lobes of the brain.

Addiction Is Addiction

I mentioned that the dopamine systems don't work well in addiction, that they become damaged. This damage, as well as frontal lobe damage, can be shown with brain scans, such as functional MRI, PET, and SPECT scans. Recent brain scan studies have not only shown abnormalities in cases of cocaine addiction, but also in cases of pathologic gambling and overeating leading to obesity.

So non-biased science is telling us that addiction is present when there is continued destructive behavior in spite of adverse consequences. As stated in the journal Science, "as far as the brain is concerned, a reward's a reward, regardless of whether it comes from a chemical or an experience."
What about pornography and sexual addiction? Dr. Eric Nestler, head of neuroscience research at Mount Cedar Sinai in New York and one of the most respected addiction scientists in the world, published a paper in the journal *Nature Neuroscience* in 2005 titled "Is there a common pathway for addiction?" In this paper he said that the dopamine reward systems mediate not only drug addiction, but also "natural addictions (that is, compulsive consumption of natural rewards) such as pathological overeating, pathological gambling, and sexual addictions."

The prestigious Royal Society of London, founded in the 1660s, publishes the longest-running scientific journal in the world, *Philosophical Transactions of the Royal Society*. A recent issue devoted 17 articles to the current understanding of addiction. Interestingly, two of the articles were specifically concerned with natural addiction, pathologic gambling and overeating.

Frantic Learning

Drs. Robert Malenka and Julie Kauer, in a landmark paper in *Nature* in 2007 on mechanisms of the physical and chemical changes that occur in the brain cells of addicted individuals, said, "Addiction represents a pathological, yet powerful form of learning and memory." We now call these changes in brain cells "long term potentiation" and "long term depression," and speak of the brain as being plastic, or subject to change and re-wiring.

Dr. Norman Doidge, a neurologist at Columbia, in his book *The Brain That Changes Itself,* describes how pornography causes re-wiring of the neural circuits. He notes that in a study of men viewing internet pornography, the men looked "uncannily" like rats pushing the lever to receive cocaine in the experimental Skinner boxes. Like the addicted rats, the men were desperately seeking the next fix, clicking the mouse just as the rats pushed the lever.

Pornography addiction is frantic learning, and perhaps this is why many who have struggled with multiple addictions report that it was the hardest for them to overcome. Drug addictions, while powerful, are more passive in a "thinking" kind of way, whereas pornography viewing, especially on the internet, is a much more active process neurologically. The constant searching for and evaluating of each image or video clip for its potency and effect is an exercise in neuronal learning, limited only by the progressively rewired brain. Curiosities are thus fused into compulsions, and the need for a larger dopamine fix can drive the person from soft-core to hard-core to child pornography—and worse. A paper published in the *Journal of Family Violence* in 2009 revealed that 85 percent of men arrested for child pornography had also physically abused children.

Dehumanized Sexuality

In addition to cortical hypofrontality and downgrading of the mesolimbic dopaminergic systems, a third element appears to be important in pornography and sexual addiction. Oxytocin and vasopressin are important hormones in the brain with regard to physically performing sexually. Studies show that oxytocin is also important in increasing trust in humans, in emotional bonding between sexual mates, and in parental bonding. We are wired to bond to the object of our sexuality.

It is a good thing when this bonding occurs in a committed marriage relationship, but there is a dark side. When sexual gratification occurs in the context of pornography use, it can result in the formation of a virtual mistress of sorts. Dr. Victor Cline, in his essay, "Pornography's Effects on Adult and Child," describes this process as follows:

> In my experience as a sexual therapist, any individual who regularly masturbates to pornography is at risk of becoming, in time, a sexual addict, as well as conditioning himself into having a sexual deviancy and/or disturbing a bonded relationship with a spouse or girlfriend.
>
> A frequent side effect is that it also dramatically reduces their capacity to love (e.g., it results in a marked dissociation of sex from friendship, affection, caring, and other normal healthy emotions and traits which help marital relationships). Their sexual side becomes in a sense dehumanized. Many of them develop an "alien ego state" (or dark side), whose core is antisocial lust devoid of most values.
>
> In time, the "high" obtained from masturbating to pornography becomes more important than real life relationships. . . .
>
> The process of masturbatory conditioning is inexorable and does not spontaneously remiss. The course of this illness may be slow and is nearly always hidden from

view. It is usually a secret part of the man's life, and like a cancer, it keeps growing and spreading. It rarely ever reverses itself, and it is also very difficult to treat and heal. Denial on the part of the male addict and refusal to confront the problem are typical and predictable, and this almost always leads to marital or couple disharmony, sometimes divorce and sometimes the breaking up of other intimate relationships.

Dr. Doidge notes,"Pornographers promise healthy pleasure and a release from sexual tension, but what they often deliver is addiction, and an eventual decrease in pleasure. Paradoxically, the male patients I worked with often craved pornography but didn't like it." In the book *Pornified*, Pamela Paul gives numerous examples of this, and describes one person who decided to limit his pornography use, not from a moralist or guilt-based perspective, but out of a desire to again experience pleasure in actual physical relationships with women.

"Porn impotence," where the man experiences sexuality preferentially with porn instead of a woman, is a real and growing phenomenon. When a man's sex drive has been diverted away from his spouse in this way, writes Dr. Cline, the wife can "easily sense this, and often [feels] very lonely and rejected."

An article in the *Journal of Sex and Marital Therapy* described a study showing that many women view the pornographic activities of their partners "as a form of infidelity":

> The theme that runs through their letters is that the man has taken the most intimate aspect of the relationship, sexuality, which is supposed to express the bond of love between the couple and

be confined exclusively to the relationship, and shared it with countless fantasy women. The vast majority of women in this study used words such as "betrayal," "cheating," and "affair " to describe the significance that their partner's involvement in pornography had for them.

A Triple Hook

Let me use a fishing analogy to illustrate some of these concepts. Every August, if possible, I try to be on the Unalakleet River in Alaska fishing for silver salmon. We use a particular lure, a triple hook called the Blue Fox pixie. As fisherman know, it is important to keep the drag loose just after hooking the fish, when it still has a lot of fight. As the fish tires, though, we tighten the drag and increase the resistance. In this way the fish is reeled into the boat and netted.

Similarly, pornography is a triple hook, consisting of cortical hypofrontality, dopaminergic downgrading, and oxytocin/vasopressin bonding. Each of these hooks is powerful, and they are synergistic. Pornography sets its hooks very quickly and deeply, and as the addiction progresses, it progressively tightens the dopamine drag until there is no more play in the line. The person is drawn ever closer to the boat, and the waiting net.

Demographic Disaster

Why is it essential to understand the addictive nature of pornography? Because if we view it as merely a bad habit, and do not afford those seeking healing the full support needed to overcome any true addiction, we will continue to be disappointed, as individuals and as a society. Pornography is the fabric used to weave a tapestry of sexual permissiveness that undermines the very foundation of society. Biologically, it destroys the ability of a population to sustain itself. It is a demographic disaster.

The author Tom Wolfe said, "The bigger pornography gets, the lower the birthrate becomes." Does he have a point? In the 1950s every country now in the European Union had a fertility rate above the 2.1 needed to sustain a population. Now none of them do, and several are at or near the 1.3 rate called the "lowest low fertility," from which it is virtually impossible to recover. It was in the late 1960s and early 1970s that this decline began, which corresponds precisely with the dawning of the sexual revolution. There is a direct correlation between the growing cultural dominance of the sexual revolution and the diminishing birthrate, and while causation may not be proven, it is strongly supported by the pheromone effect of pornography.

Demographic decline is, of course, multi-factorial. Urbanization, women in the workplace, gender role adaptation, and even increased life expectancy are important factors in the inverted population pyramids. But the primordial, or biological factors of human sexuality and family stability are primary and, in my opinion, haven't been appropriately weighted.

In 1934 Cambridge anthropologist Dr. J. D. Unwin published *Sex and Culture*. In it he examined 86 cultures spanning 5,000 years with regard to the effects of both sexual restraint and sexual abandon. His perspective was strictly secular, and his findings were not based in moralistic dogma. He found, without exception, that cultures that practiced strict monogamy in marital bonds exhibited what he called creative social energy, and reached the zenith of production. Cultures that had no restraint on sexuality, without exception, deteriorated into mediocrity and chaos. In Houposia, *The Sexual and*

Economic Foundations of a New Society, published posthumously, he summarized:

> In human records, there is no instance of a society retaining its energy after a complete new generation has inherited a tradition which does not insist on pre-nuptial and post-nuptial continence. . . . The evidence is that in the past a class has risen to a position of political dominance because of its great energy and that at the period of its rising, its sexual regulations have always been strict. It has retained its energy and dominated the society so long as its sexual regulations have demanded both pre-nuptial and post-nuptial continence. . . .

I know of no exceptions to these rules.

Pornography as Flamethrower

Unwin also described what may be called "dopaminergic distraction," where pleasure-seeking dominates and productivity is diminished. Will Durant, in *The Lessons of History*, wrote that "sex is a river of fire that must be banked and cooled by a hundred restraints if it is not to consume in chaos both the individual and the group."

If "sex is a river of fire," dopamine and other brain drugs are the fuel. Like the astronauts of Apollo 11, we can ride this energy to the heavens, or be consumed in its exhaust, depending on whether we are above the engines in the command module or underneath them, thus exposed to the heat. Dr. Henry A. Bowman said, "No really intelligent person will burn a cathedral to fry an egg, even to satisfy a ravenous appetite," yet the flamethrower of pornography is torching many cathedrals of marital, parental, and familial love today.

I applaud ongoing efforts to strengthen laws, but in our current legal and social environment, we cannot depend upon the government for restraint. We must face the reality that pornography will affect virtually every family in some way. Dr. Jason Carroll and his colleagues published a widely cited paper in the *Journal of Adolescent Research* that brings to light the scope of this problem. According to this paper, which reviewed data from five universities, 87 percent of college males and 31 percent of females view pornography. This data crosses all religious, educational, and social barriers.

Pornography has become the sex education venue for the majority of the next generation, an internet candy store, and it teaches that sex is physically and emotionally harmless, with no negative consequences. Men and women are mere visual drugs to be used and discarded, and sex is solely for personal pleasure. The truth, of course, it that those who actually perform sexually to make the pornography are consumed and discarded by pornographers; they are "throwaway people," as Dr. C. Everett Koop called them.

Help for Healing

Dr. John Mark Chaney's description of teenage pornography addiction is equally true for adults:

> Professionals sometimes fail to understand the power of the compulsion youth are facing, and it is not uncommon for school, religious, or private-sector professionals to advocate a simple treatment plan that is based upon willpower or moral character. Since pornography can be an addiction, these "just say no" types of approaches are likely to only create more frustration and self-defeating ideation . . . the intervention and treatment modality must recognize

the problem as a full addiction, and treat it with the same consideration given to alcohol or chemical substances.

Regarding healing, Dr Victor Cline says,

> I have found that there are four major factors that most predict success in recovery. First, the individual must be personally motivated to be free of his addiction and possess a willingness to do whatever it takes to achieve success. . . . You can never force a person to get well if he doesn't want to. . . . Second, it is necessary to create a safe environment, which drastically reduces access to porn and other sexual triggers. . . . Third, he should affiliate with a twelve-step support group. . . . Fourth, the individual needs to select a counselor/therapist who has had special training and success in treating sexual addictions.

Let us reach out with understanding to those already trapped, who live in shame and secrecy. Shaming them will not heal them. As Jeffery R. Holland said when he was president of Brigham Young University, "When a battered, weary swimmer tries valiantly to get back to shore, after having fought strong winds and rough waves which he should never have challenged in the first place, those of us who might have had better judgment, or perhaps just better luck, ought not to row out to his side, beat him with our oars, and shove his head back underwater."

Secular philosophy will not heal them either, and the government can't save them. Step 2 of the Twelve-Step program for sex addicts says that those healed "came to believe that a Power greater than [themselves] could restore [them] to sanity." Interestingly, peer-reviewed studies support the success of Twelve-Step programs, which are based on the aid of a Higher Power.

Indeed, Unwin's research, conducted from a secular perspective, demonstrated that all advanced societies studied, when at their cultural and productive apices, built temples to whatever gods they worshiped. It was in this subjugation of the secular to the sacred, of the limbic to the lobe, that they peaked in their self-control and, therefore, in their self-determination. Will Durant, who described himself as agnostic, also found that "there is no moral substitute" for religion in providing this tempering of the limbic.

The Battle Is Joined

Pornography is a drug that produces an addictive neurochemical trap, "past reason hunted, and no sooner had, past reason hated," as Shakespeare put it in Sonnet 129. And yes, as we have seen, ice cream and sexuality can be akin to crack cocaine.

While we must continue to fight the good fight legally and societally, we are way beyond avoidance as our only defense. Pornography wants you, it wants your husband or wife, it wants your son and daughter, your grandchildren, and your in-laws. It doesn't share well, and it doesn't leave easily. It is a cruel master, and seeks more slaves.

Abraham Lincoln, when he faced a similar war over freedom, said, "If all do not join now to save the good old ship of the Union this voyage nobody will have a chance to pilot her on another voyage." All hands on deck. The battle is on for sanity and serenity, for peace and prosperity, for today, and for all our tomorrows.

Chapter 15: Obsessive Compulsion

When you get to the point where you can no longer tell your flesh no, you're in some serious trouble. It's a spirit of lasciviousness. Your behavior in certain areas will become excessive, but they will also become obsessive. This behavioral pattern is not limited to your sexual practices, though that will be the area in which it is most noticeable and the most prevalent. Regardless of how and what you feed your flesh, the fact remains that you're feeding it, and everything is connected.

In addition to my addiction to pornography, I also battled addictions to food and video games. When I was in college, I would spend 10 hours a day playing Halo 2 on Xbox Live. When I wasn't playing Xbox I was watching porn. When I wasn't watching porn I was having sex. When I wasn't having sex I was getting high or drunk. You see the pattern? Your flesh will indulge and gorge itself on *anything* that you allow it to.

At that point in my life I was especially vulnerable to addictive behaviors because of my circumstances. In August of 2004, I had gastric bypass surgery. Therefore, I was literally incapable of physically feeding my flesh and indulging my gluttonous habits the way I was accustomed to. That's when my gaming habits got out of control. Some experts call the phenomenon "transfer addiction." It's a condition in which an obese, food addict has a life and body altering surgery making them physically unable to feed that addiction the way they normally would. At that point those addictive behaviors would morph, translate, or manifest themselves in another form or fashion. I've met people in my weight loss support groups who had gastric bypass surgery, lost a lot of weight, and then became sex addicts, drug addicts, alcoholics, kleptomaniacs, cutters, hypochondriacs, anorexic, OCD.....you name it, I saw it. These people had one of their addictions taken away, but the root of the problem was never discovered and destroyed, so the destructive behaviors started to manifest themselves in other forms. There were also those, who lost a lot of weight because of the surgery, then gained most if not all of the weight back a few years later when their stomach began to stretch back to normal. I fell into that category. After losing 86lbs in the first six months, my old eating habits and desires started to come back. I hit a plateau for about a year, then I started gradually creeping back up. After a couple of years I had gained back about 60lbs of the 86lbs that I had originally lost. Getting the surgery was like trying to kill weeds with a pair of scissors. If you cut the leaves off, it appears that the problem has been dealt with. Sure, you couldn't see it anymore, but without killing the root, it is bound to come back.

Chapter 16: Unrealistic Expectations

In case you're just now figuring it out, porn is a fantasy. Porn is not real life. It's a cheap, unrealistic depiction of sexual interactions. The biggest problem with this is that it causes you to start seeing things from that angle. Most of the women you see in mainstream studio porn are more luscious and seductive than the women you deal with in real life. If you couple that with the power of makeup, airbrushing, and strategic lighting you've got women who appear to be sexually perfect. In addition, a porn actress will do things on screen that most men's wives would scoff at. When you continually feed your spirit with this unhealthy and unnatural depiction of sex, you're going to develop unrealistic expectations. You will come to a point where your wife no longer satisfies you because she won't do anal, or because she won't swallow, or because she's a B cup and not a triple D. You see what I'm getting at? The women you see in porn are the most self-loathing, self-hating, insecure, and emotionally unstable people in the world. But on screen, they portray themselves as goddesses. On screen they seem willing and even down right eager to do all of the nasty, raunchy things that you could ever fantasize about, but in real life they're defiled women being paid for their services. It's all an act. The people at XXXChurch and The Pink Cross have shared many testimonies of women who were involved in the porn industry, women who later became saved and told about all of the horrific atrocities they dealt with. Those women aren't happy. In many cases, they're performing on screen for money to feed some other kind of addiction.

It is imperative that you begin to understand that what you see on screen is not real. In porn, you'll see the cable guy come over and within a minute or two he and the unsuspecting housewife are enjoying a romp in the sack. These scenes that we consistently indulge ourselves in are missing many key ingredients of a healthy sexual relationship. Obviously, the interacting parties aren't married, so it's a sin from the start. But most porn, unless it's softcore porn written and directed by a woman, rarely includes any elements of romance. In addition, when it comes to foreplay, it's usually dramatically biased to the male receiving pleasure and not the female. This depiction is selfish and it's unhealthy. When you see these scenes over and over and over again, you begin to think that this is how sex is supposed to work. You'll start believing that your needs should be met right now, and her needs are irrelevant.

Anyone who's been married longer than five minutes knows that this idea won't fly with the Mrs.

Porn will give you the idea that women are as easily stimulated as we are, and that's simply not the case. A woman needs time and effort, romance and foreplay, loving and tenderness to be brought to arousal. As men, we usually only need a stiff breeze on a cool day to get excited. When it comes to sexual arousal, men are like microwaves while women are like crock pots. *Selah.*

Look at it this way: porn is an equal opportunist. The dangers and side effects of porn aren't limited to men alone. Yes, the majority of regular porn viewers are men, but studies have shown that the percentage of female viewers has been dramatically increasing over the past few years. Imagine that you married a woman who was a porn addict. Your initial reaction might be excitement because you're thinking if she's a regular viewer that she might do a better job of living up to your fantasies. Though I can certainly understand the point of view, I think the argument and philosophy are rather short-sighted. A female porn addict is going to have the same problems as her male counterparts, but they would probably manifest themselves in a different manor. For example, a female porn viewer will develop unrealistic expectations as well. If a woman were to indulge in watching porn on a regular basis, she may be inclined to think that there's something wrong with a man who isn't as endowed as Jake Steed, Nacho Vidal, or Lexington Steele. How would you feel if your wife was disappointed with your endowment because she thinks that she needs double-digit inches to be satisfied? That would leave most of us coming up short, literally. Again, it's an unrealistic fantasy. It's not real life. And the longer you keep putting that filth in your spirit, the further and further up the creek you're going to drift.

The side effects of unrealistic expectations and sexual frustration are mutually exclusive. They go hand in hand. When your expectations are unjustifiably and unrealistically high, you're bound to become frustrated when your sexual experiences in life don't live up to the porn-fueled fantasies you desire. All of my sexual experiences that occurred before I was walking in my deliverance were a let down.

I had this crazy notion that once I got married I was going to have sex non-stop. I thought that marriage was going to be a 24/7 orgy and that my wife was going to be an insatiable sex kitten. I later realized that this idea was a result of years and years of porno consumption. Not only did porn give me an unrealistic view of my future wife and our sexual relationship, it also distorted my view of myself. I thought that my sex drive was abnormal. I thought that I was some sort of freak. I know now that this was another one of Satan's lies. Porn had taken my natural God-given sex drive and perverted it into something abnormal and uncontrollable. It was like Dr. Jekyl and Mr. Hyde.

After breaking free from the bondage and influence of lust and pornography, I discovered that my natural sex drive was healthy and normal. I didn't *have* to have sex everyday as a married man. Sex is an important part of a healthy marriage, but it's just that, a part. There's far more to a good marriage than sexual gratification. Unfortunately, a large number of Christian men who have fallen into the snares of porn enter into the marriage covenant disillusioned and distracted. As a result, they are starting their marriages off on the wrong foot and slowly but surely losing the affections of their brides.

Chapter 17: Sexual Dysfunction

Sexual dysfunction is closely related to sexual frustration. You could even say that one's sexual dysfunction could cause sexual frustration. As formerly mentioned, all of these side effects are closely related to one another. While the previous section talked specifically about how ones unrealistic expectations led to sexual frustration due to unfulfilling sexual experiences, this section will deal with some of the physical and mental aspects of a person's sexual function and performance that can and will be dramatically affected by continual porn consumption.

Though this topic of sexual function and performance is for the married men (because if you're not married you shouldn't be "performing" sexually at all), it's important for the unmarried men (and boys) to pay close attention because they need to understand and learn this as well. The human sexual response is broken down into four stages: arousal, plateau, climax, and recovery.

One of the biggest misconceptions about masturbation is that it builds up your sexual endurance (plateau). This is the idea that repeated and habitual masturbation will allow you to have sex for longer periods of time because your penis is used to continual friction. Back when I was living in sin, I was a firm believer in this idea. However, I've come to learn that this is completely and utterly untrue. In fact, the opposite is actually correct. Frequent and habitual masturbation actually lowers your sexual endurance and causes you to reach orgasm much faster. Allow me to explain. Masturbation is selfish. The sole purpose of masturbation is to meet your own sexual needs. Sexual endurance is irrelevant when you're masturbating, and most tend to masturbate quickly in order to reach their climactic destination. So, while the act of masturbation feels good along the way, the objective is the orgasm. Self-stimulation puts too much emphasis on the climax and minimal emphasis on the plateau. During masturbation, a lot of men go from arousal to orgasm so fast that the plateau stage is almost completely ignored. This can be dangerous because women need considerably more time at the plateau stage in order to reach climax. There are, however, exceptions to this rule. Many times in my past, I used to try and delay my orgasm for long periods of time, but this was only because I wanted to consume as much porn as possible before my orgasm. In fact, I would argue that it wasn't the plateau stage at all, rather, it was an extended arousal period. I can attest to this because many times while I was watching porn, I wouldn't masturbate until I was somewhat mentally satisfied with the amount of porn I had consumed. Many times, this would be hours after I started watching porn. But the psychological/emotional "satisfaction" never lasted, because when I was done masturbating I'd start the process over again. Again, lust can never be quenched.

Over time, you begin to condition your body to this response. We are creatures of habit, and many times we're unaware of the negative habits we're developing with our daily routine. So while you may think masturbating builds up your sexual endurance, it is in fact tearing it down, making your orgasms arrive sooner than planned while having sex. This will leave your wife rather unsatisfied which could in turn have negative effects on your ego and self-esteem, not to mention her self-esteem. If you are habitually consuming porn, your wife alone cannot and will not "satisfy" you visually and sexually the way you think porn can. So, you won't be as willing to prolong the sexual experience to ensure her satisfaction because you're going to be too focused on your own orgasm. You may be willing to do it during masturbation, because it's all about YOU and your visual/emotional arousal, but because that same level of arousal won't be there with your wife (if you're a regular porn user – and this has nothing to do with her. This is a result of YOUR porn consumption.) you're selfishness will kick into high gear and you'll completely and totally neglect her satisfaction.

In addiction to this physical dysfunction, there are also spiritual and emotional components that lead to a dysfunctional sexual experience. If you're a Christian involved in pornography, masturbation, and/or fornication, you've taken something that God designed to be beautiful and defiled it. That doesn't come without a price. Over the years, my sexual behavior caused me to develop a sinful view of all things sexual. This didn't just disappear the moment I got married. In fact, it took a good 4-6 months of being married before I was fully able to enjoy sex with a clear conscience.

In the beginning stages of our marriage, it was very hard for me to "stay focused" when having sex with my wife. I had spent 16 years of my life living in a sexual fantasy world. Even after repenting of my sin and walking away from porn and lust forever, it was difficult to purge my mind of all of the lustful images I had consumed over the years. This made it difficult for me to stay in the moment with my wife while we made love. My mind tended to wander and drift, and I had to continually force myself to stay focused. In those early stages it was hard to close my eyes while sexually engaging my wife because images and such would pop into my head without my permission. This was a result of so much porn consumption. Later in the book we'll discuss how to handle those sorts of thoughts and images.

Chapter 18: Objectifying Women

I remember seeing news video of feminist organizations protesting porn studios and companies. I took note when I observed that the majority of women doing the protesting were homely and unattractive and I remember thinking, "You're just jealous because no one wants *you* to take your clothes off." Though that may be true in some sense, the chief concern of the protestors is a valid one. Porn objectifies women. There's no denying it. There's no way to sidestep or dance around the truth. It's as simple as that. A man addicted to porn is like a junkie waiting on his next fix. In his case, women are the objects of his obsession.

When you buy into the fantasy life that porn has you subscribe to, you begin to lose the ability to view women as people. In your mind, you don't view them as human beings. You view them as a means to an end – the end being your own sexual satisfaction and gratification. This is never more apparent than in the time some have referred to as basking in the afterglow. I can recall sexual encounters that I had while I was living in sin. I remember how the state of my mind completely changed a few seconds after my orgasm had subsided. What just happened? Thirty seconds ago, this moment was the highlight of my day, and a few moments afterwards I was absolutely disgusted. I remember hooking up with women that I didn't find attractive. Why? Because it was an easy conquest, and it was a means to an end. At the time, it all made sense to me. I didn't care about their dreams, their desires, or their ambitions. I wasn't concerned with their political views, their family history, or what they were looking for in a guy. I was only concerned about one thing, and I knew exactly what to say and what to do to get it. I was a wolf in sheep's clothing. I had this twisted idea that God put women here for my enjoyment.

My eyes were out of control. I literally checked out every woman I saw. I would ogle them from a distance and wonder what they looked like naked. I wondered what they were like in bed. I'd imagine that they all secretly wanted me. It didn't matter whether they were young or old, fat or skinny, tall or short. I started to covet. The things I saw became the things that I wanted. I had mastered the art of sneaking glances. I didn't realize that every peak and every glance I took was like a mental snapshot. Those images were cataloged and filed deep within my subconscious. They were part of the fuel that grew the fires of lust within me that triggered my compulsive behavior.

Chapter 19: The Jezebel Effect

As you well know, there are many different forms of sexual immorality. There are those that are specifically listed out in the bible: fornication, homosexuality, adultery, beastiality, incest, pedophilia, and the like. There are also those like masturbation and sexual fantasies that are alluded to and inferred but aren't specifically mentioned. If you're like me, you probably took the legalistic road to justify your sin. Know this: Satan is a liar. It's what he does. It's pretty much all he knows how to do. And since he knows the scriptures better than most believers, he has an uncanny ability to twist the Word just enough that it sounds right but has completely lost its effectiveness. For me, I bought into the lie that watching porn, having sexual fantasies and masturbating were the lesser of two evils. My flesh argued that my getting myself off to porn was better than going out and having sex, so it was really the only option that I had. Not only was it a lie, but it was a double-edged lie; it was two-fold. It was a lie because God doesn't believe in alternative sin. He doesn't believe that a sin substitution is the way to go. It's not like substituting Splenda for real sugar to make your cookies less fattening. That kind of legalism doesn't fly with God. The other part of the lie rests in the fact that I actually believed that watching porn and masturbating would keep me from having sex, when in actuality it was pushing me towards it.

God is a seed God. When you plant seeds, you are going to get a harvest – whether they were good or bad seeds. When you plant seeds of lust via porn, masturbation, and sexual fantasies, you are eventually going to reap a harvest. Often times that harvest will come in the form of a sexual compulsion like fornication or adultery. There are some whose porn consumption has progressed so much that they've developed an appetite for child pornography, which in turn creates a desire for sexual relationships with children. As mentioned in the previous article, 85% of people arrested for child pornography had abused children at some point. Let's see what the Word says about it, because you're not obligated to take anything I or anyone else says as gospel, if it's not backed up in the scriptures.

> *Blessed is the man who endures temptation; for when he has been approved, he will receive the crown of life which the Lord has promised to those who love Him. Let no one say when he is tempted, "I am tempted by God";*

for God cannot be tempted by evil, nor does He Himself tempt anyone. But each one is tempted when he is drawn away by his own desires and enticed. Then, when desire has conceived, it gives birth to sin; and sin, when it is full-grown, brings forth death.

James 1:12-15

If you think that you can feed your flesh continually and not eventually act out on it, you're fooling yourself. Those seeds have been conceived in your spirit and will eventually manifest themselves into a sexually compulsive behavior. In our technologically driven society, porn is just the tip of the iceberg. There are other social formats like MySpace, Facebook, AIM, and Yahoo that have the potential to morph into a breeding ground for one's lustful desires.

The biblical definition of sexual immorality is receiving sexual pleasure, satisfaction, or gratification absent of your spouse. If you're using one of the aforementioned social outlets to cultivate inappropriate relationships with people, you're walking outside of the will of God. I know of men (and women) who would flirt and have sexually explicit conversations behind their spouse's back with people on MySpace, Facebook, Skype, or Chat Roulette. Some would even engage in sexual behaviors like sending or receiving nude/inappropriate photos and/or masturbating or watching someone masturbate via webcam. Then, they would have the audacity to say that they weren't cheating because they didn't physically do anything with the other person. This is in spite of the fact that Jesus said that whoever looks at a woman (person) lustfully has already committed adultery with them in his heart. That's another prime example of the legalistic nature of our flesh.

Chapter 20: Impartation

According to Webster's dictionary the word *impart* is a transitive verb. It means to give, to convey or to grant from. It also means to communicate the knowledge of. Impartation is noun that receives the transaction. When a person or people are involved in sexual immorality, there is always an impartation of some sort. Most people are well aware of the possible or even inevitable forms of physical impartation. These could include viruses and/or infections. The results of a physical impartation could also be a pregnancy. When a man imparts or gives his seed to a woman, the designed result is a baby. That's how God designed human beings to procreate. The transfer of seed results in new life.

When people engage in sexual activity, a spiritual impartation also occurs. This too was part of God's design. Marriage is a covenant. It's sad that our society has diminished its purpose to merely a legal contract. Despite what society says, God designed marriage to be a blood covenant. Many biblical scholars believe that the reason women are born with a hymen is because when she's penetrated by her husband for the first time, it is supposed to symbolize the blood covenant that Christ shares with the church. You also need to keep in mind that in today's American society, women are getting married much later in life and most virgins past the age of sixteen or seventeen don't have their hymens in tact due to tampon use and/or medical exams. That doesn't nullify the reason God put it there or invalidate the meaning of its symbolism.

When a man and a woman engage in sexual intercourse, God views them as one flesh. This is how we were designed. The problem with this situation is that if the two people are not married, they are not rightfully partaking in the experience. This poses a tremendous problem for the two, whether they're aware of it or not.

Throughout the text of the Bible, there are only a few things that God describes as holy. A few examples are the Holiest of Holies in His temple, the tithe, and our bodies – that is if you have accepted Jesus as your Lord and Savior. Whenever you misuse or violate something that God deems as holy, you do so at your own peril. God is very clear and specific. There are consequences for your disobedience. This still applies whether your disobedience is intentional or not. There are many Christians who violate God's Word without even knowing that they are doing so. According to the Bible, ignorance is not an excuse for disobedience. God clearly says in Hosea 4:6 that His people perish and are destroyed for lack of knowledge. It's been said that what you don't know can't hurt you. That's the lie of all lies, because what you don't know can kill you. You might not know the importance of tithing because of what your church does or does not teach. But if you're not paying your tithes, the Bible clearly says that you're cursed with a curse, because you're robbing God. That applies whether you're doing it knowingly or not.

The same concept applies for sexual immorality. God has declared that our bodies are holy because they're the temple of the Holy Spirit. So when you violate God's Word by defiling your temple, you are stepping out from underneath God's umbrella of protection and leaving yourself vulnerable to Satan's attacks. We talked briefly about some of the physical consequences of sexual immorality, but it's extremely important for you to understand the spiritual consequences as well.

Back to impartation: there is an undeniable spiritual transfer that occurs as a result of sexual intercourse. Much like anything else, this was something that God designed for our good, but Satan has twisted it in order to harm us. When two become one physically through the act of sexual intercourse, their spirits are joined as well. In the context of marriage, this is a beautiful thing with tremendous spiritual symbolism. A man and his wife share the most intimate part of one another. However, when this occurs outside of God's will, then the process will bring harm upon the partakers. The Apostle Paul talks about it in 1 Corinthians 6 when he says:

> Do you not know that your bodies are members of Christ? Shall I then take the members of Christ and make them members of a harlot? Certainly not! Or do you not know that he who is joined to a harlot is one body with her? For "the two," He says, "shall become one flesh." But he who is joined to the Lord is one spirit with Him. Flee sexual immorality. Every sin that a man does is outside the body, but he who commits sexual immorality sins against his own body. Or do you not know that your body is the temple of the Holy Spirit who is in you, whom you have from God, and you are not your own? For you were bought at a price; therefore

glorify God in your body and in your spirit, which are God's.

1 Corinthians 6:15-20

When you become one with someone who is not your spouse, the spiritual impartation can be devastating. Part of them becomes part of you. This means that everything that they struggle with, whether it is an addiction, a compulsion, or a behavior, has the ability to transfer over to you. It gets even worse if you're engaging in sexual activity with a person who is under the influence or possession of demonic spirits. All of a sudden, getting laid doesn't sound too appealing does it?

Jesus confirmed this concept in John chapter 4 in His encounter with the Samaritan woman at the well. He was telling her about living water, and He asked her to call her husband to bring the man to Him. She then told Him that she didn't have a husband, to which Jesus replied, *"You have well said, 'I have no husband,' for you have had five husbands, and the one whom you now have is not your husband; in that you spoke truly."* Jesus was explaining to her that despite her not being married, the men she was sleeping with were considered her husbands according to God because of their physical union.

If you have engaged in sexual activities with someone other than your spouse, you need to repent. In addition, you need to ask God to break the spiritual yokes that have bound you to that person spiritually and physically. You may still be reaping the harvest of seeds you planted years ago without even knowing it. This is not something that should be taken lightly. If it's important to God, it should be important to you.

The effects of impartation do not end there. A man's seed holds the blueprint for the next generation. I've heard about extremely selective sperm banks that administer IQ tests and consider one's appearance before allowing him to make a donation. Then, when someone wants to purchase the sperm later down the road, the bank can sell the customer on the fact that the donor was a Harvard graduate and dashingly handsome. The same concept applies with breeding horses. The genes have the ability to reproduce after their own kind. The previous examples are solely physical, but there's a similar impartation going on spiritually.

Whatever a man struggles with will be passed along to his seed, unless he has received his deliverance from God and chooses to continually walk in it. This is a spiritual principle. How many times has a frustrated mother shouted "You're just like your father!" in a fit of rage to her son? It's not coincidence. Why do you think Jesus could not be born from a man's seed? Joseph was a good man, but sin still coursed through his blood. He got it from his father, and he got it from his father before him. It's an ongoing cycle, and it can only end intentionally. This is not something that just goes away. This is not solely in regards to sexual sins either. How many men struggle with the same health problems their fathers and grandfathers struggled with? You might say, "Diabetes runs in my family." That may be true, but gluttony and lack of self control were in your family long before diabetes showed up. *My people perish for lack of knowledge.*

You are going to have to face Daddy's demons at some point. If you're struggling with an addiction to lust and pornography, it's more than likely your father struggled with the same thing – at least up until you were conceived, and that behavior was imparted to you via his seed. I remember a time when my father caught me watching porn online in my room. I was about twenty at the time. It was one of those father son talks that you really weren't comfortable having, but, I later realized that it was necessary. Through tears, my dad apologized to me for what he had given me. He went on to tell me about how he struggled with porn up until the time that I was a young boy, but had since received his deliverance. He also told me about how when he was young he had found my grandfather's stash of dirty magazines.

You didn't have any control of the hand you were dealt in life. The good news is that you have the power, ability, and responsibility to correct the issue now to prevent future generations from being dealt the same hand. This doesn't have to continue, but you need to make the choice to do the right thing. If you don't have children, there's still time for you to fix it before passing it along. If you've already passed it along, your child can still be aware of the hand he's been dealt. Knowing what you're pre-disposed to can go a long way in preventing addiction from ever developing.

Chapter 21: Liar, Liar, Pants on Fire

Depending on a person's situation, this may or may not be an issue for them. If your environment and circumstances provide no sort of accountability in regards to your porn viewing, then you may not ever have issues with lying. However, if you're like me and you had people in your life who were attempting to keep you accountable, it's possible, even likely, that you'll fall victim to these demoralizing side effects.

Lying is a slippery slope. For most people, lying starts off as something small. It's not really seen as a big deal because we argue that the *little white lies* don't really hurt anyone. Sometimes it's convenient. Sometimes it gets us out of a jam. Sometimes it spares a person's feelings. Even if that's true, there are still consequences for that kind of behavior. The Bible says that God *hates* lying. In fact, when it lists the six things that God hates, lying is listed twice. If that's not an exclamation point, I don't know what is.

> *These six things the Lord hates, yes, seven are an abomination to Him: a proud look, a **lying** tongue, hands that shed innocent blood, a heart that devises wicked plans, feet that are swift in running to evil, a false witness who speaks **lies**, and one who sows discord amongst the brethren.*
> Proverbs 6:16-19

Selah. Pause and think about that for a moment. Here is God speaking through Solomon and He gives six things that He hates and seven things that are an abomination to Him and he lists lying *twice.* Now, I'm not a seminary trained Bible scholar, but even I can see the significance of these verses. The Bible says in 1 Corinthians 13:1 and Deuteronomy 19:15 that everything must be established by the mouth of two or three witnesses. I, like many Christians, believe that when God is trying to get something across to us through his Word, it can be found in the scriptures more than once. How much more emphatic is it when the two witnesses to establish the principle are within the same chapter, a couple of verses apart?

Since it has been established that God hates lying and that it's an abomination to Him, let's look at some of the consequences that can occur because of this particular action. I believe that lying is a form of pride and selfishness. Whenever you see a person that lies often, you'll probably see them embody those other traits as well. As previously stated, habitual lying usually starts off as something small. Then, over time, if the person is successful in their subtle attempts at dishonesty, the behavior begins to spread like an undetected cancer. Where the person was once lying occasionally about things that mattered, now they're lying frequently about things of little consequence. Like most deviant behaviors, lying becomes an addiction.

When a person becomes a habitual liar, they start to lose sight of who they are as an individual. Why? Because they've lost themselves in the fabricated details. A little lie here, an embellishment there, soon the person can't tell the truth and reality from the fantasy world they've created with their own lies. They become delusional. They start believing their own lies. Don't believe me? Consider this: people will believe just about anything if they hear it enough. During the 2008 election cycle, all of the "objective" news sources talked about how bad the economy was. That was the story that drove the election. The collapse of wall street started to affect main street. Every where you turned, that's all you would hear. Now, was the economy actually slowing down? Absolutely. Was it as bad as it was being portrayed on TV? Certainly not, at least not at that time. If it was, it wouldn't have taken me all day to find a parking spot at the mall the week of Christmas. When it's a true recession/depression, people stop spending money, but somehow every time I made it to a retail location during the Christmas season, it was jam packed. How in the world could people spend money on recreation during "the greatest economic crisis facing America since the Great Depression?" Perhaps the crisis wasn't as bad as it was made out to be. But, most people believed it because they heard it repeatedly.

People who lie function the same way. They fabricate the details of their lives, their past, and themselves. Eventually, they can't tell where their lies end and the truth begins. This relates to porn the way it relates to just about any other addiction. A person with an addiction to porn starts off in denial. Denial is the first form of lying, because when you're in denial, you're lying to yourself. When you're unwilling to admit to yourself how bad the problem is, it's very unlikely that you're going to take any steps to improve the situation. After all, why would I try to fix a problem that I don't believe exists?

Many times when you're dealing with an accountability partner, a spouse, or even a significant other, lying feels like a viable option. Do not allow yourself to fall into that trap the way that I did. When you're dealing with an addiction to porn, keeping secrets comes naturally. You don't want anyone to know about your dirty little private moments. That feeling is magnified ten-fold when you're dealing with someone of the opposite sex. During my struggle, it was easier for me to tell my father than it was for me to tell Jess. Obviously, I felt this way for a number of reasons, some of which may not be applicable to your situation. But the biggest reason is because she took it personally. She felt like I was drawn to porn, because I wasn't attracted to her or that she wasn't enough to satisfy me. Truth be told it really had nothing to do with her (I will talk more about this later). This was something that I had struggled with long before I knew her. But the fact that I knew how she viewed the situation made it incredibly difficult for me to be honest. When you find yourself in a situation where it's difficult to be open and honest, your integrity is going to be challenged. I found this out the hard way.

Because of my habitual pattern of lying, I developed a strong sense of paranoia. The truth comes naturally. Because the details of the truth are what really happened, it really shouldn't take much effort to recall and remember those details. Lying, embellishment, and fabrication take effort. You have to consciously remember the truth, and choose to go in another direction. When you're dealing with friends, loved ones, associates, or people that you spend time with on a regular basis, this can be especially dangerous. When you speak lies, it takes a lot of thought and effort to remember them; this is increasingly true when you tell different lies to different people about the same events or circumstances. Then, you have to remember what you told to whom. This becomes exponentially difficult. When you find yourself trapped in a prison of your own lies, as I did, paranoia is inevitable. This is true because exposure is your greatest fear. I had been dating Jess for over a year before she really knew who I was, and even then there were still certain caverns and caves within my secret soul that I had not privileged her to.

When you fear being exposed, you're constantly looking over your shoulder. You become irritable, abrasive, and defensive. When I had fallen off the wagon and gone back into looking at porn, the same was true for me. I knew I had messed up, but I was afraid to tell the truth and face the music. So I made the decision either consciously or subconsciously (I'm not quite sure) to keep up the behavior until I got caught. On the surface, I dreaded the thought of being exposed, because I knew what was at stake, but deep down inside I think I wanted to get caught. I was tired of living a double life. It's a miserable existence when your conscience is continually trying to convict you, and you persist on ignoring it. I couldn't even look myself in the mirror without being disgusted by who and what I had become. I repeated this pattern countless times in my life. I couldn't see that Satan had me in bondage. I was a slave to my own flesh. The Bible says that a double-minded man is unstable in all of his ways (James 1:8). I think God had me in mind when He wrote that.

Chapter 22: It's All About Me, Me, Me, Me, Me

I personally believe that selfishness and impatience are siblings. Think about it. When you lack patience, it's usually because you personally believe that your time is more valuable than the time of everyone else. That's a pretty selfish attitude in my opinion. Though they are closely related, there are other factors that promote the individual behaviors. For example, I think that our society as a whole is very impatient. We have technology to thank for that. When I was in middle school, and we had to write research papers, it meant spending countless hours at the library researching a topic thoroughly enough to be able to intelligently write a thesis. Now, kids have the internet. Our microwave, gotta have it now, generation has lost the importance and the virtue of being patience. Why spend the time to peel, boil, and mash your own potatoes when you can buy instant potatoes in a box and just add water? Why grind your own coffee beans and wait for them to roast and brew when you can pay $5 and have a pimple-faced barista make your drink for you? Don't get me wrong. Technology is great. The problem is that we come to expect everything to be instant. Some things take time. But we want what we want, and we want it right now. That attitude has scarred our culture. Instead of men taking the time, effort, and commitment to pursue a woman, love her, cherish her, and marry her, we would rather figure out the quickest way into her panties. No matter how you look at it, it always leads back to selfishness and impatience.

I got hooked on porn during the explosions of Pay-Per-View and the internet, so I'm especially aware of instant gratification. Several years ago people had to go to dark and dirty porn shops and/or theaters to get their fix. Now, it only takes a few clicks of the mouse. Masturbation is the quintessential form of selfishness. No one else's needs matter to you. All you care about is getting yourself off, usually at any cost. When you're caught up in this behavior habitually, you'll begin to see that your own selfishness and impatience are not mutually exclusive to your sexual behavior. Regardless of *how* you became a self-absorbed, selfish, and impatient person; the fact remains, that's what you've become. I was one who had to be in control. I wanted to be in charge. When I took leadership roles at school or work, people admired me. They thought it was because I had the best interest of everyone in mind, when in actuality I only cared about my own success, and I didn't trust anyone else with it.

I had spent years of my life meeting my own needs whenever I felt like it. I had trained and conditioned myself to only look after my own interests. That kind of deep-rooted selfishness caused many problems in my relationship with Jess. Even to this day, fully walking in my deliverance from porn and lust, I still struggle with being selfish. The only difference is that now I'm aware of it. I know that I can have selfish tendencies at times, so I'm open and receptive when my wife comes to me in a loving manner and says she think I'm being a little selfish about something.

Chapter 23: Emotional Detachment

As I previously pointed out, sex was designed to be a gift from God to married couples. It's meant for procreation as well as recreation. Sex was designed to be a spiritual union as well as a physical one. When a person indulges in porn they are setting themselves up to put far too much importance on the physical components of sex while generally ignoring the spiritual and emotional aspects of this great experience. The results of said behaviors are emotional detachment and incompetence (the inability to meet the emotional needs of another person).

Again, a lot of these side effects blend together. You can say this one is closely related to selfishness, and I would have to agree with you. Porn makes you focus on the visual stimuli. You don't see romance. You don't see the emotional aspect of sex. You don't see all of the work that goes into making and keeping your wife happy. All you see is the physical part. This is such a problem, because you're so well-versed in the anatomical requirements that you're completely ignorant to a woman's emotional needs.

At the time I got married, I had been abstinent and porn/masturbation free for nearly 100 days. After the first 30 days or so, my sex drive had pretty much dried up. I wasn't feeding my flesh *anything,* so it was very easy to control the occasional urge. As the wedding approached, it seemed that the desires started to intensify. I think it's safe to chalk it up to sheer anticipation. Despite my natural, God-given desires, I was able to keep my flesh under control and walk in sexual purity.

Jess and I were legally married in our [then] pastor's office the morning of our wedding date (we've since changed churches). Our pastor had a prior engagement and couldn't make it to the ceremony. We had planned to have our marital counselor to perform the traditional ceremony that evening. Our first sexual encounter as a married couple was about an hour or so after we left our pastor's office. Since the day was upon us, I felt as though I couldn't wait any longer. My beautiful bride shared my feelings, and we were united as husband and wife shortly thereafter. The sexual bliss that I thought I had found came to an abrupt halt a few days after the honeymoon, when Jess told me that she was getting frustrated with our sex life.

The next few months were difficult. Don't get me wrong, I was getting my physical needs met, but I always felt that Jess was doing it out of obligation and fear. She felt obligated because she was my wife and that was one of her responsibilities, but she did it out of fear because she was afraid that if she withheld that I'd fall back into porn (or perhaps would go running back to it). It was like we were stuck in a rut. She felt like a vagina in a glass case, "break glass in case of emergency." It was heartbreaking to hear her tell me that she felt replaceable, that any woman could trade places with her, bend over and meet my needs, and it wouldn't make any difference to me. That's how she felt.

I spent a lot of time in prayer and in the Word trying to find a solution. During that time, Holy Spirit revealed a number of things to me – most of which were very humbling. First He showed me that I was having difficulty connecting sex and love as a result of my prior porn addiction. My wife was trying to use sex as an expression of her love, and I was using sex as an expression of my hormones. Sex, in my view, was solely for meeting a need. It's like eating plain oatmeal. Yes, it will prevent you from starving, but it isn't very good. Your belly is full, but you're not satisfied. Couple that with the fact that it was like my wife had an entire delicious dinner prepared that she wanted to share with me so that I could meet the need *and* enjoy the process, but I was refusing and merely settling for just getting by. That revelation was pretty painful, but it was helpful nonetheless.

Holy Spirit also showed me that I was putting too much emphasis on the sexual experience and not enough emphasis on meeting my wife's emotional needs. I learned that if I put the time in and met her emotional needs, she'd give me more sex than I could handle. But if I focused on my physical needs first, her needs would go unmet, and the sexual experience would be unfulfilling for both of us.

The last, and probably most valuable thing, He revealed to me is the fact that sex *is* very important to my wife; we just stressed its importance differently. I expressed its importance through frequency. I wanted sex often, as most men do. She expressed its importance through quality. It didn't matter how often we made love, as long it was an enjoyable experience for her and she climaxed too. It's like go 100% or don't go at all. Once she got the engine warmed up, it was frustrating and disappointing when she didn't get to finish. I thought about how mad/frustrated I'd be if I made sure she had gotten off and she rolled over and went to sleep without considering my needs. I realized then that I wasn't being fair to her. After that, I repented my selfishness to her and asked God to help me to be more attentive to her needs. Our sex life has dramatically improved since then and is mutually fulfilling.

Chapter 24: Roid Rage

This ties in closely with selfishness and impatience. The anger portion of this side effect can be triggered by a number of things. I've found in my experience that one of the biggest triggers for anger is a person who's trying to hold you accountable and will persist at asking probing questions when you're trying to hide something. Accountability is necessary and should trigger unrighteous anger at times when it's done right. When your sinful nature is trying to prevent being exposed, it's going to signal an angry response. Though it's contrary to what you want at that moment, it's good for you – especially when you're aware of why it's happening. That anger is rooted in your own personal selfishness and lack of patience. It's understandable, but it's not justifiably acceptable. This is a response of the flesh, and if you're currently in that boat, your flesh is far more dominant than you're spirit at this point. That's okay; well, it's not okay but it's part of the process, and we're going to work on that; but you need to be aware of it. Part of walking in the flesh is being controlled by your emotions. Emotions make great slaves, but they make horrible masters. When you learn to walk in the spirit, you will be in complete control of your emotions. They will become your servants and you can use a healthy emotional response to motivate you to do the right thing. However, when your emotions rule, they will cause an unhealthy response that will cause you to act outside the will of God and eventually sin.

Your consumption of porn may not end with anger. For certain people it can certainly progress into violence. Ted Bundy, one of the most notorious serial killers and rapists in American history explained how his involvement with pornography gradually led him down the path to rape and murder. He conducted an interview with Dr. James Dobson from Focus on the Family the day before he was slated to be executed. The following is the transcript from that interview:

James C. Dobson: It is about 2:30 in the afternoon. You are scheduled to be executed tomorrow morning at 7:00, if you don't receive another stay. What is going through your mind? What thoughts have you had in these last few days?

Ted: I won't kid you to say it is something I feel I'm in control of or have come to terms with. It's a moment-by-moment thing. Sometimes I feel very tranquil and other times I don't feel tranquil at all. What's going through my mind right now is to use the minutes and hours I have left as fruitfully as possible. It helps to live in the moment, in the essence that we use it productively. Right now I'm feeling calm, in large part because I'm here with you.

JCD: For the record, you are guilty of killing many women and girls.

Ted: Yes, that's true.

JCD: How did it happen? Take me back. What are the antecedents of the behavior that we've seen? You were raised in what you consider to be a healthy home. You were not physically, sexually, or emotionally abused.

Ted: No. And that's part of the tragedy of this whole situation. I grew up in a wonderful home with two dedicated and loving parents, as one of 5 brothers and sisters. We, as children, were the focus of my parent's lives. We regularly attended church. My parents did not drink or smoke or gamble. There was no physical abuse or fighting in the home.
I'm not saying it was "Leave it to Beaver", but it was a fine, solid Christian home. I hope no one will try to take the easy way out of this and accuse my family of contributing to this. I know, and I'm trying to tell you as honestly as I know how, what happened. As a young boy of 12 or 13, I encountered, outside the home, in the local grocery and drug stores, softcore pornography. Young boys explore the sideways and byways of their neighborhoods, and in our neighborhood, people would dump the garbage. From time to time, we would come across books of a harder nature - more graphic. This also included detective magazines, etc., and I want to emphasize this. The most damaging kind of pornography - and I'm talking from hard, real, personal experience - is that that involves violence and sexual violence. The wedding of those two forces - as I know only too well - brings about behavior that is too terrible to describe.

JCD: Walk me through that. What was going on in your mind at that time?

Ted: Before we go any further, it is important to me that people believe what I'm saying.

I'm not blaming pornography. I'm not saying it caused me to go out and do certain things. I take full responsibility for all the things that I've done. That's not the question here. The issue is how this kind of literature contributed and helped mold and shape the kinds of violent behavior.

JCD: It fueled your fantasies.

Ted: In the beginning, it fuels this kind of thought process. Then, at a certain time, it is instrumental in crystallizing it, making it into something that is almost a separate entity inside.

JCD: You had gone about as far as you could go in your own fantasy life, with printed material, photos, videos, etc., and then there was the urge to take that step over to a physical event.

Ted: Once you become addicted to it, and I look at this as a kind of addiction, you look for more potent, more explicit, more graphic kinds of material. Like an addiction, you keep craving something which is harder and gives you a greater sense of excitement, until you reach the point where the pornography only goes so far - that jumping off point where you begin to think maybe actually doing it will give you that which is just beyond reading about it and looking at it.

JCD: How long did you stay at that point before you actually assaulted someone?

Ted: A couple of years. I was dealing with very strong inhibitions against criminal and violent behavior. That had been conditioned and bred into me from my neighborhood, environment, church, and schools. I knew it was wrong to think about it, and certainly, to do it was wrong. I was on the edge, and the last vestiges of restraint were being tested constantly, and assailed through the kind of fantasy life that was fueled, largely, by pornography.

JCD: Do you remember what pushed you over that edge? Do you remember the decision to "go for it"? Do you remember where you decided to throw caution to the wind?

Ted: It's a very difficult thing to describe - the sensation of reaching that point where
I knew I couldn't control it anymore. The barriers I had learned as a child were not enough to hold me back from seeking out and harming somebody.

JCD: Would it be accurate to call that a sexual frenzy?

Ted: That's one way to describe it - a compulsion, a building up of this destructive energy. Another fact I haven't mentioned is the use of alcohol. In conjunction with my exposure to pornography, alcohol reduced my inhibitions and pornography eroded them further.

JCD: After you committed your first murder, what was the emotional effect? What happened in the days after that?

Ted: Even all these years later, it is difficult to talk about. Reliving it through talking about it is difficult to say the least, but I want you to understand what happened. It was like coming out of some horrible trance or dream. I can only liken it to (and I don't want to over-dramatize it) being possessed by something so awful and alien, and the next morning waking up and remembering what happened and realizing that, in the eyes of the law, and certainly in the eyes of God, you're responsible. To wake up in the morning and realize what I had done with a clear mind, with all my essential moral and ethical feelings intact, absolutely horrified me.

JCD: You hadn't known you were capable of that before?

Ted: There is no way to describe the brutal urge to do that, and once it has been satisfied, or spent, and that energy level recedes, I became myself again. Basically, I was a normal person. I wasn't some guy hanging out in bars, or a bum. I wasn't a pervert in the sense that people look at somebody and say, "I know there's something wrong with him." I was a normal person. I had good friends. I led a normal life, except for this one, small but very potent and destructive segment that I kept very secret and close to myself. Those of us who have been so influenced by violence in the media, particularly pornographic violence, are not some kind of inherent monsters. We are your sons and husbands. We grew up in regular families. Pornography can reach in and snatch a kid out of any house today. It snatched me out of my home 20 or 30 years ago. As diligent as my parents were, and they were diligent in protecting their children, and as good a Christian home as we had, there is no protection against the kinds of influences that are loose in a society that tolerates....

JCD: Outside these walls, there are several hundred reporters that wanted to talk to you, and you asked me to come because you had something you wanted to say. You feel that hardcore pornography, and the door to it, softcore pornography, is doing untold damage to other people and causing other women to be abused and killed the way you did.

Ted: I'm no social scientist, and I don't pretend to believe what John Q. Citizen thinks about this, but I've lived in prison for a long time now, and I've met a lot of men who were motivated to commit violence. Without exception, every one of them was deeply involved in pornography - deeply consumed by the addiction. The F.B.I.'s own study on serial homicide shows that the most common interest among serial killers is pornography. It's true.

JCD: What would your life have been like without that influence?

Ted: I know it would have been far better, not just for me, but for a lot of other people - victims and families. There's no question that it would have been a better life. I'm absolutely certain it would not have involved this kind of violence.

JCD: If I were able to ask the kind of questions that are being asked, one would be, "Are you thinking about all those victims and their families that are so wounded? Years later, their lives aren't normal. They will never be normal. Is there remorse?"

Ted: I know people will accuse me of being self-serving, but through God's help, I have been able to come to the point, much too late, where I can feel the hurt and the pain I am responsible for. Yes. Absolutely! During the past few days, myself and a number of investigators have been talking about unsolved cases - murders I was involved in. It's hard to talk about all these years later, because it revives all the terrible feelings and thoughts that I have steadfastly and diligently dealt with - I think successfully. It has been reopened and I have felt the pain and the horror of that. I hope that those who I have caused so much grief, even if they don't believe my expression of sorrow, will believe what I'm saying now; there are those loose in their towns and communities, like me, whose dangerous impulses are being fueled, day in and day out, by violence in the media in its various forms - particularly sexualized violence. What scares me is when I see that's on cable T.V. Some of the violence in the movies that come into homes today is stuff they wouldn't show in X-rated adult theatres 30 years ago.

JCD: The slasher movies?

Ted: That is the most graphic violence on screen, especially when children are unattended or unaware that they could be a Ted Bundy; that they could have a predisposition to that kind of behavior.

JCD: One of the final murders you committed was 12-year-old Kimberly Leach. I think the public outcry is greater there because an innocent child was taken from a playground.
What did you feel after that? Were they the normal emotions after that?

Ted: I can't really talk about that right now. It's too painful. I would like to be able to convey to you what that experience is like, but I won't be able to talk about that. I can't begin to understand the pain that the parents of these children and young women that I have harmed feel. And I can't restore much to them, if anything. I won't pretend to, and
I don't even expect them to forgive me. I'm not asking for it. That kind of forgiveness is of God; if they have it, they have it, and if they don't, maybe they'll find it someday.

JCD: Do you deserve the punishment the state has inflicted upon you?

Ted: That's a very good question. I don't want to die; I won't kid you. I deserve, certainly, the most extreme punishment society has. And I think society deserves to be protected from me and from others like me. That's for sure. What I hope will come of our discussion is that I think society deserves to be protected from itself. As we have been talking, there are forces at loose in this country, especially this kind of violent pornography, where, on one hand, well-meaning people will condemn the behavior of a Ted Bundy while they're walking past a magazine rack full of the very kinds of things that send young kids down the road to being Ted Bundys. That's the irony. I'm talking about going beyond retribution, which is what people want with me. There is no way in the world that killing me is going to restore those beautiful children to their parents and correct and soothe the pain. But there are lots of other kids playing in streets around the country today who are going to be dead tomorrow, and the next day, because other young people are reading and seeing the kinds of things that are available in the media today.

JCD: There is tremendous cynicism about you on the outside, I suppose, for good reason.
I'm not sure there's anything you could say that people would believe, yet you told me (and I have heard this through our mutual friend, John Tanner) that you have accepted the forgiveness of Jesus Christ and are a follower and believer in Him. Do you draw strength from that as you approach these final hours?

Ted: I do. I can't say that being in the Valley of the Shadow of Death is something I've become all that accustomed to, and that I'm strong and nothing's bothering me. It's no fun. It gets kind of lonely, yet I have to remind myself that every one of us will go through this someday in one way or another.

JCD: It's appointed unto man.

Ted: Countless millions who have walked this earth before us have gone through this, so this is just an experience we all share.

One of the things that I find most interesting is the results of the F.B.I study that showed the only common thread between ALL serial killers is an obsession and addiction to pornography. Regardless of race, gender, sexual preference, or targeted victims, all of them had an affinity for porn. Even serial killers that didn't rape their victims were tangled up in the web of lust and pornography.

Now, does this mean that all porn addicts will turn into murderers? Certainly not. But, you have to be aware of what it's capable of in order to truly know what you're getting yourself into. Not all people who choose to smoke die of lung cancer, but that doesn't mean that smoking is any less dangerous, right?

Chapter 25: The Golden Member

When I hear the word idol, the first thing I think about are the idols of the Old Testament – Baal, the golden calf, things of that nature. Truth be told, an idol is anything that takes a higher priority in your life than God. It doesn't have to be a statue or a figure of another god, it can be something that appears as harmless as video games, television, or one's physical appearance. The Bible is very clear that God is jealous. He's very jealous, and He has every right to be. His greatest passion and desire is to have a personal relationship with us. He wants fellowship, and He despises anything that prevents that from happening. This is specific to individuals on a case by case basis. Something that acts as an idol in your life may not be an idol in mine. This means that there are things that in and of themselves may not be harmful and thus despised by God in my life – like television, but if you spend eight hours a day in front of the boob tube and don't spend any time with God, He will have problems with your excessive use of TV. Does that make sense?

Take food as another example. Food in and of itself is not bad. We need food for sustenance. However, to the glutton, food is an idol. It's made its way from sustenance to a source of pleasure to a complete and total obsession. The glutton doesn't get on his hands and knees and bow in worship to food (at least I hope not), but his constant obsession, attention and service can easily be seen as an act of worship. I'm quite sure that's how God views it.

Lust and porn consumption are even worse. Whereas food has a natural use and healthy application, lust and porn have no place in the believer's life whatsoever. But, your flesh takes it a step further. Not only does it crave and desire something it shouldn't have at all, but when you continue to feed it those desires, it will continue to obsess and long for more. Like a fire that will consume anything in its wake and require more, your flesh has every intention of doing the same. At that point you're dealing with idolatry and God is very jealous.

When you continue in a lifestyle obsessed with your own sexual gratification, you've made an idol out of your flesh and every act of lust, perversion, masturbation and gratification is an act of worship. You're cheating on God. You're essentially telling him "Thanks for sending your son to die for me. I know He died to deliver me from this, but I enjoy this too much to give it up, and quite frankly You're not as important to me as my penis." Granted, you might not have those conscious thoughts, but you might as well. That's essentially what you're telling God when you choose to worship your flesh as opposed to worshipping Him.

Imagine how much more fulfilling your life would be if you replaced all the time you spend looking at porn and masturbating with prayer, reading your Bible and spending quality time with your Father. How much of your life has porn taken? You think you're consuming porn, but it's actually consuming you. I know I've personally spent the time equivalent of at least a year or two feeding my flesh. I've spent countless hours watching porn. I've masturbated thousands of times. And what has it gotten me? I wish I could have that time back, but I can't. I have to look forward knowing that God has forgiven me and cleansed me of those past deeds and has used my flaws to help others. That's my testimony. I left the altar of sexual idolatry, knelt down at God's feet, and haven't looked back. What will you choose to do?

Chapter 26: Improper Validation

Men need to be validated. God designed masculinity to be bestowed from one generation to the next. This process involves a man who actively initiates a boy. It's not done by accident. It has to be intentional. Boys long to be the apple of their father's eye. They want to know they're strong and powerful and have what it takes. When a child doesn't get this emotional and psychological need met, it leaves him scarred. Although it's ideal to receive validation from one's natural father, it can be given by any older male that has influence in the child's life – a grandfather, uncle, pastor, neighbor, mentor, etc.

This information is very important to know, because we live in a society that has been attacking masculinity for decades now. We're seeing more and more men who were raised by mothers due to the emotional or physical absence of their fathers. Often times this results in a boy trapped in a man's body. He has physically grown up, but he hasn't emotionally or psychologically been initiated into manhood and therefore has a number of important questions that haven't been answered. Do I have what it takes? Am I strong? Am I powerful? How do I handle adversity? How do I handle disappointment? What if I fail? There are so many questions.

When left unanswered, these questions don't just go away. They will haunt a man for his entire life. When that happens, you find men who are continually searching for that validation that they never got from Daddy. This leaves a man vulnerable to the attacks of the enemy. Society will tell you that nothing makes a man feel like a man more than a woman. In the wrong context an invalidated man will look to women for that validation. This is a critical error. Women were never meant to be the source of your strength and validation. Rather, they were meant to find security in it. When you look for strength and validation in a woman, you will always be disappointed. That's not their role, and trying to put that responsibility on them negatively affects everyone involved. It's like a wife who tries to find emotional security and companionship in her son because her husband doesn't meet her need. That's not his responsibility and trying to pin that on him will damage him as well as the mother.

As always, porn magnifies this problem. The majority of porn is targeted towards male viewers. It doesn't get anymore obvious than that. If you're a man seeking validation, porn will undoubtedly lead you astray. You see the seductive women on screen, and you fantasize about them desiring you. With porn, they are always readily available to you whenever you want or need them. Superficially, this seems to fill that void and answer those questions. She makes you feel like you have what it takes. She makes you feel like a real man. You begin to think that being a real man is all about knowing how to sexually please a woman, and when you believe that, you've completely missed the mark. You may not realize then how much damage is being done, but eventually you will inevitably begin to see how that false validation prohibits you from being emotionally available to a real woman in the context of a relationship. This is because no real validation had ever taken place. It was a façade – a smokescreen. As Denzel Washington said while playing *Malcolm X*, "You've been hoodwinked, bamboozled."

For more information about masculine initiation and validation I would highly recommend reading *Wild at Heart* and *The Way of the Wild Heart* by John Eldredge. These topics can barely be exhausted in a book, let alone a few paragraphs. I think all men should read them, but especially those described in this chapter. The knowledge and information made available in these wonderful books will definitely change your life.

Chapter 27: Collateral Damage

Many women feel as though a man who's watching pornography isn't being faithful. I tend to agree with that idea. When you consume pornography, you are allowing yourself to be sexually aroused by someone other than your wife, which is completely contrary to God's definition of sexual purity. In fact, Jesus spoke directly about this idea in Matthew 5:28 when he said that anyone who so much as looks at a woman lustfully has already committed adultery in his heart. There's absolutely no way to rationalize or legalize your way around the facts. When you watch porn you are being aroused by and lusting after fantasy women. By definition, this is infidelity.

How do you think that makes your wife feel? Hurt? Angry? Betrayed? Inadequate? Fat? Unattractive? Yes. That's exactly how it makes her feel. The sad truth is that your wife cannot compete with porn. Period. She just can't. She wasn't meant to. She was supposed to have your complete and total attention, but by bringing that baggage into your marriage bed, you're unconsciously making her compete in a situation where she has no shot at winning. It's like the winless Detroit Lions of 2008 playing the undefeated Patriots of 2007 (well, undefeated until the Super Bowl. Yeah, I hate the Patriots too).

The fact that she cannot compete isn't her fault though. It's the nature of porn. Porn allows you to indulge your fantasies and curiosities in ways that weren't possible in the past, especially with the use of the internet. With the click of a button you can watch fat women, skinny women, old women, young women, tall women, short women, blondes, redheads, brunettes, cheerleaders, nurses, housewives, children, trannies, men, animals.... The list goes on and on. During your consumption, you're developing unhealthy and unnatural attractions and cravings for things that your wife cannot fulfill. She cannot be all of those things at once, but porn can.

So your consumption of pornography is rendering her own, natural, God-given beauty inadequate. The fact that you weren't intending to have this effect on her is irrelevant. It is what it is. Even the most confident and self-secured woman would have her confidence shattered under these conditions. Women begin to take this personally. When I was watching porn, I never understood why it was so painful to Jess. She kept telling me that it made her feel inadequate. At the time, I couldn't see the damage I was causing. I didn't think my porn consumption had anything to do with her. I had been watching porn since I was ten, and I didn't meet Jess until I was twenty four. I couldn't possibly connect the dots as to how it was about her since I was a user long before we met. Little did I know that it was a bit of a self-fulfilling prophecy.

She thought the cause of my watching porn was rooted in my being displeased or dissatisfied with her physically. Though that wasn't the cause, it was certainly the result. Allow me to explain. I didn't sit down and think, "Man, I'm really not happy with how she looks, so I think I'll watch porn to supplement my arousal." But, the more porn I consumed, the less and less pleased I was with her physically.

Porn isn't real. It's a fantasy portrayed by actual people that's been scripted and edited and cleaned up so much that it gives and unrealistic and unhealthy depiction of a sexual relationship. Most of the women in studio porn are flawless. Generally they're busty, lusty, willing, and wet. After continual consumption, this will cause a man to think that there's something wrong with his bride if she's not the same. When in fact there's nothing wrong with her. The problem is your perception. You're holding her to a standard that isn't real.

What you don't see in porn is all of the "behind the scenes" things that go into creating that fantasy. You don't see the guys popping Viagra and being "fluffed" between scenes so they can stay erect. You don't see the women being waxed, plucked, shaven, and made-up by teams of professionals to portray the illusion of perfection. You don't see the director and editors using PhotoShop to edit, hide, and correct every possible blemish and imperfection on the performers' bodies. You don't see them using lube by the bottle to ease the pain from chafing and bleeding caused by unnatural amounts of friction for extended periods of time. You don't see the cut scenes where the women are vomiting from being forced to deepthroat an actors' 9 incher. You don't see them crying and bleeding from an anal sex gangbang because while the cameras are rolling they're all smiles and moans. You don't see that the 15 minutes scene you're watching could've taken six hours to shoot. Do you have any idea how uncomfortable and painful it is to have sex for nearly six hours straight? There's a lot that you don't see. You see the end result, but you have no idea how they got there. Porn stars are actors. They act like they like it. They act like it's pleasurable. They act like it's the best thing in the world. But it's just that – an act.

I would recommend you visit www.thepinkcross.org to see the truth about porn. You need to know what these people are going through to create your fantasy. It's not glamorous, and it's certainly not pretty, but it's the truth, and the truth will make you free.

My years and years of consumption took their toll on my perception. I got to the point where I wasn't satisfied with Jess. I felt that her B cup breasts weren't ideal and that I "deserved" bigger. I was a real jerk. I tried to pressure her into getting a boob job so that she could better fulfill my porn-influenced fantasies about what I thought was ideal. I wanted her breasts to be bigger, I wanted her to be thinner, I wanted her to shave a certain way, I wanted her to do certain things in the bedroom, and so on. How do you think that made her feel? Even though I'm not longer that person, it makes me sick to my stomach when I think about all of the things that I put her through because of MY problem. I didn't love her for who God made her, and it was causing more damage than I could've ever imagined.

Three years into my deliverance, Jess started this workout planned called Russian Kettlebell, and in less than a year, she lost about 70lbs. She went from a size 18 to a size 8. As she approached her goal weight, she came to me and asked me about my thoughts on her getting a boob job. You can imagine my hesitation. I didn't want to touch that subject with a 10 foot pole – not after all I had put her through in the past. Then, she explained to me how she was happy with 99% of her body, but she was still unhappy about her breasts and that she wanted to be more proportional. At 6' tall and a size 8 with wide hips, her breasts were noticeably small on her frame, so she wore padded bras and additional inserts that we affectionately called her "chicken cutlets," since that's what they looked like.

I had to walk a tight rope here. I told her that I didn't want her doing this for me. I was content. But, if she wanted to do it for her, I would support her. This was a very challenging time for me. Even though she assured me she was doing it for herself, I still felt bad. I think I felt bad because I found myself getting excited thinking about her with bigger boobs, but I didn't want her doing something like this solely for my enjoyment.

After the surgery and recovery, I know this was the right decision for my wife. Her confidence has exploded. Now, I am not saying that there's something wrong with small breasts or that every woman needs to consider getting a boob job – not at all. This was the right choice for us. If your wife is confident and happy with what she has, you should be too. If you're facing this issue in your marriage, you should definitely pray about it and come to an agreement as a couple.

Chapter 28: Separation from God

In my opinion, this is one of the most devastating side effects to porn consumption. It's a category in and of itself, but there are also a number of subcategories that fall under its umbrella. The reason separation from God is so catastrophic is because God designed us for fellowship with Him. Every other side effect previously listed could partially be a result from your being separated from God. Why? Because a genuine personal relationship with the Father can and will keep you from sin. Yeah, it really is that easy. As I began my journey, my motivation to not sin was the mentality that I couldn't. Now, it's because I don't want to. I am so inseparably close to my Father that I don't want to sin, and my desire to please Him fuels my resolve and steadfast spirit to keep me walking in my deliverance. In the same manner that my love for my wife will ensure that my actions and lifestyle will never put me in a position to stray from her or the vows I committed to, my love for my Father keeps me walking that straight and narrow to assure that I'm always faithful to Him.

When Adam and Eve sinned, they developed a sin consciousness. They were able to know right from wrong. They were no longer naïve. For that reason, the law was implement a few hundred years later, because even though people had the internal knowledge of right and wrong, there was no specific standard that people could be held to. Once the law was established, the standard was in place, but people still didn't have the power to fully live up to God's expectations. Again, the purpose of the law was to set the standard and give people a path and direction to follow; but living up to that standard was incredible hard. In the New Testament there are many references to the curse of the law, because the law itself brought bondage. Because of the law, people developed a strong sense of legalism, which then led to discussions about the spirit vs. the letter of the law.

Jesus came to change all of that. His fulfilling of the law meant that we no longer had to live under it anymore. Rather, we live by grace, and have liberty from the curse of the law. Well, what exactly does that mean? It means that in order to be free from sin, we need to know that we are free to sin. I know that sounds a bit off, but let me explain. Being free to sin means we are righteous because Jesus is righteous, and our faith in Him is our justification. Our righteousness is not dependent on our actions, but this is contrary to what the enemy would have you believe. Now, our freedom to sin doesn't mean that we should go off and unremorsefully throw ourselves into a sinful lifestyle. The Bible is very clear about that.

> *What shall we say then? Shall we continue in sin that grace may about? Certainly not. How shall we who died to sin live any longer in it? Or do you not know that as many of us were baptized into Christ Jesus were baptized into His death? Therefore we were buried with Him through baptism into death, that just as Christ was raised from the dead by the glory of the Father, even so we also should walk in newness of life.*
> Romans 6:1-4

This is the biggest difference between the old and new covenant. We have exclusive rights to new life that comes by accepting Jesus as our savior. Not only do we get new life when we die, but we're also privileged enough to get new life while still here on earth. Along with the New Covenant came the Holy Spirit. The Bible calls the Holy Spirit our Helper. He is our Enabler. He is God that lives within us, giving us the ability to walk uprightly, not by our own strength, but by God's. Now you know it's possible. Later in the book we'll talk about how to access the power to cause the change that will bring about new life. Although new life on earth is a gift, most believers don't know how to accept it and break free from the old life. I'm going to show you how.

The Bible calls Satan the accuser of the brethren. He's continually pointing out our flaws in an attempt to condemn us. The reason he does this is because he knows that God won't. Granted, one of Holy Spirit's jobs is to convict us when we sin, but this is not to condemn us. We need to understand that there's a big difference between conviction and condemnation. Conviction by Holy Spirit is for correctional purposes. It is to impress upon your spirit that you have done something that does not align with the will of God. It's God's way of correcting us.

> *My son, do not despise the chastening of the Lord, nor detest His correction; for whom the Lord loves He corrects, just as a father the son in whom he delights.*
> Proverbs 3:11-12

Condemnation is completely different. It expresses adverse judgment against a person and proclaims them to be guilty.

> *There is therefore now no condemnation to those who are in Christ Jesus, who do not walk according to the flesh, but according to the Spirit.*
> Romans 8:1

The Bible says that if you're in Christ, there is no condemnation; yet the enemy is constantly trying day in and day out to condemn us for our wrong doings. He knows that human nature inherently expresses cowardice. When Adam and Eve sinned, they hid from God. When Jonah didn't want to carry out his assignment, he hid from God. When you step back and think about it, it really sounds foolish, doesn't it? How can you hide from God? Though these Biblical examples tried to hide themselves physically, it's still rather prophetic, because we tend to do the same thing spiritually. When we sin, we have a habit of hiding from God. This was my personal experience. Whenever I fell off the wagon so to speak, I generally fell hard. The combination of guilt, sorrow, disappointment, and self pity was a recipe for disaster. I had this mindset that since I had fallen back into sin, I might as well take my time repenting. It was almost as if I had to sin more in order to feel REALLY bad about it and want to come back to God, but it never worked out that way. The more I would sin, the further and further I would drift. Usually, I would avoid church, stop praying, and essentially ignore God as if He wasn't there. This is exactly what Satan wants. That's the entire purpose of his condemnation. When we receive his condemnation, we tend to walk away from God. A wolf can only snag a sheep if the Shepherd isn't around, and we know that whenever God isn't around, it's not because He left. He said He'd never leave us nor forsake us. If we find ourselves away from the presence of God, it's because we've walked away.

When we're separated from God, we have no power, no peace, and no protection. The Bible says that in His presence there is fullness of joy. When you operate in the Kingdom of God, or God's way of doing things, you are covered by His umbrella. Underneath that umbrella are life, liberty, peace, and protection. So when you stray from Him, and walk out from under that covering, you're essentially on your own.

A few years back we learned about the horrific details of the Steve McNair murder-suicide case. As a Baltimore Ravens fan, this hit especially close to home for me. Here was a man who professed Christ, but was having multiple affairs with a number of different women, one of whom ended up taking his life before taking her own. It's a very tragic story. My heart breaks for McNair's family. Imagine what his wife was going through. It's bad enough to get a call from the police saying your husband was murdered, shot in the head twice and the body twice, but to find out at that moment that he was having an affair as well had to have been devastating. How does a person digest that? Imagine how his four children felt. His sin and disobedience directly led to his demise. If he had his flesh under control and followed the order of the One he professed, he would still be alive. Instead, he walked in the flesh, stepped outside of the will of God and from underneath that covering; and it cost him his life.

This brings up another common discussion in the church: can one lose his or her salvation? Personally, I do not believe that a person can unintentionally lose their salvation like one loses his house keys. But I do think that you can purposely choose (either subtly or blatantly) to walk away from God, thus rendering your salvation useless. I believe that the condition of the heart is critical. Because we didn't earn our salvation with works, I think it's impossible to lose our salvation through works. It's not as though we have a sin bank that gives us our "allowance" of sins, and God cuts us off when we've used them all. That's preposterous. However, I do believe that if you walk in habitual sin without regret or remorse (enough to make you repent and turn away), that you're treading on thin ice.

You can look at a number of Jesus' parable for confirmation. Jesus used parables to relay a spiritual truth by expressing it in common everyday situations. This format is both complex and yet surprisingly simple. It allows His audience to get the initial point rather quickly, while having enough density and substance to allow more review and study of the subject matter to reveal more hidden truth. Take the Prodigal Son for example. This parable deals with man's inherent, albeit foolish desire for independence and God's never-ending forgiveness. The son asks for his inheritance and leaves his father's house to go off on his own. While out on his own, he squanders his money, his morals, and his life on cheap thrills and fast living. By the time he comes to his senses, he decides that it's best he go home in hopes that his father will accept him back as a servant. While he's still a long way off, his father runs to him and greets him, kisses him, and puts a nice garment on him. A great party ensues as the father says "My son who was once dead, is now alive." This statement is VERY prophetic. Think about the parallels to our life. I think that the Prodigal Son can represent a Christian – God's child. The son chose to leave his father's house. It was his decision. I think this can symbolize a Christian walking away from his salvation because of sin. Again, the sin itself isn't the direct cause, rather it's the condition of one's heart, which is subsequently caused by the habitual sin. What would've happened if the Prodigal Son died while off living on his own? Furthermore, what do you think happens to a Christian who dies while living apart from his salvation? The father in the story, who obviously represents God, said that his son was once dead, but now is alive. Why would God say that about His child? When you leave God, are you dead in your sin? I would guess that this is in fact what He's implying.

I believe that when we get caught in a pattern of habitual sin, we walk away from God, thus forfeiting our salvation. I have a really hard time believing the "once saved, always saved" mantra. The idea that a person can accept Jesus as his savior and then go off and live a lifestyle of sin, never acknowledging Him again, and still see heaven doesn't sit well with me. If that were the case, why would anyone want to live right? Living in sin is more gratifying from a carnal standpoint, so why follow God's word if you can do whatever you want here on earth and still die and go to heaven? If a homosexual accepts Christ as his savior, but never changes his sinful lifestyle and spends the rest of his life in habitual, sexual sin, do you think they would die and go to heaven? I have a hard time believing that. Of course, there is scriptural support to confirm my position.

> *Whoever commits sin also commits lawlessness, and sin is lawlessness. And you know that He was manifested to take away our sins and in Him there is no sin. Whoever abides in Him does not sin. Whoever sins has neither seen Him nor known Him. Little children, let no one deceive you. He who practices righteousness is righteous, just as He is righteous. He who sins is of the devil, for the devil has sinned from the beginning. For this purpose the Son of God was manifested, that He*

might destroy the works of the devil. Whoever has been
born of God does not sin, for His seed remains in him,
and he cannot sin, because he has been born of God.
1 John 3:4-9

This passage of scripture is pretty clear. When it says "commits sin" it is referring to committing habitual sin or living a sinful lifestyle. Leave it to Holy Spirit to produce a soul-piercing decree like this. If you're not convicted by this scripture, it means that you're not living in sin and therefore have nothing to be convicted of, or you're so far gone that you can't even recognize the conviction of the Holy Spirit – which in and of itself is a horrible place to find yourself.

For it pleased the Father that in Him (Jesus) all the
fullness should dwell, and by Him to reconcile all things
to Himself, by Him, whether things on earth or things in
heaven, having made peace through of the blood of His
cross. An you, who once were alienated and enemies in
your mind by wicked works, yet now He has reconciled
in the body of His flesh through death, to present you (to
God) holy, and blameless, and above reproach in His
*sight – **if indeed you continue in the faith**, grounded*
and steadfast, and are not moved away from the hope of
the gospel which you heard, which was preached to
every creature under heaven, of which I, Paul, became a
minister.
Colossians 1:19-23

The fact that Paul says "If indeed you continue in the faith" and "are not moved away from the hope of the gospel" denotes that one can, in fact, choose to not continue in faith and could possibly be moved away from the hope of the gospel. If you don't continue in faith and are moved away from the gospel of salvation, are you still saved? My guess is no.

Living in sin is serious business. When the Bible says that the wages of sin is death, it's talking about spiritual death as well as physical death. God didn't design Adam and Eve to be mortal. They were supposed to live forever, but because of sin, God had to shorten the lifespan of human beings. Think about it. What if men like Hitler,

Stalin, and Saddam Hussein were able to live forever? How much harder would life be for the rest of us if evil people didn't die?

God is our source. Every good and perfect gift comes from Him (James 1:17). Therefore, being separated from Him is the beginning of the end for us. Every living soul has a void that only God can fill. This, however, is a continual process, which is why it's so important to develop a walk with God. We need to be in constant communion with our Father, if we expect to live the best life. Are you living God's best right now?

Chapter 29: And I'm Spent

Admission is the first step to recovery. I'm trying to help map a blueprint for you so that when you begin to see this in your life, you will be reminded of what you've read. If and when that happens, it will continue to establish my credibility with you. This is vital because later in the book when I'm showing you the necessary steps you'll need to take in order to finally break free of this addiction, there are going to be a lot of things that your flesh is not going to want to do. It will do everything it can to try and convince you that "this step isn't necessary," or "I don't really need to do that." Hopefully by establishing and solidifying my credibility with these predictable responses, you'll understand and realize that I'm telling the truth.

Look at it this way. If you were lost in a place you've never been before, would you rather be lost and completely on your own, or would you want to be lost while on the phone with someone who knows the area and can tell you what to expect, what spots to avoid, and how to get back on the right track? Essentially, that's what I'm doing. I've been where you are, and I know what to expect. I want to guide you through to ensure your journey is easier than mine was.

Making the decision to break free from porn is as simple as that – making the decision. You need to know and understand that God has already done His part. When Jesus died for our sins He paid the price for our freedom. We have everything we need to walk in liberty; we just have to choose to do so. I do need to warn you, however, that even after you've made the decision not to consume porn any longer, it's going to take some time to heal from all of the negative side effects that have manifested themselves in your life. The internal change is immediate. It's like salvation in a sense. Your deliverance is a gift that Jesus provided; as soon as you choose to accept it, you're delivered. Just like that. However, you have to take the necessary steps to continue to walk in that deliverance and heal from all of the damage that's been done.

Here's another example: imagine your porn addiction as a jail cell. You feel trapped, and it appears like there's no way out. But your bail has already been paid and the door to your cell is unlocked. You have every right to open your cell door and walk out, but most people won't. There are a number of reasons why. Some people really don't want to walk away from their sin. As bad as it may sound, I'm sure many of us have been in that spot before. I know I was. I used to think that porn defined me, and I viewed a life without porn in a similar way that I viewed a life without air or food – it just couldn't be done. There are also those who don't have the spiritual instruction, faith or wherewithal to just reach out and open their cell doors. Some people don't know that it's unlocked. Some of us have been tricked by the enemy into believing that there's no escape. Maybe you're like that with porn, or gluttony, or homosexuality, or fornication. Take your pick. Our freedom has already been purchased. Our debt has already been paid. But unless we know this and choose to exercise our authority to claim what's rightfully ours, Satan will continue to hold us in bondage. Make the choice to break free right now, and I will show you how.

> *Pattern yourselves after me [follow my example], as I imitate and follow Christ (the Messiah).*
> 1 Corinthians 11:1 [Amplified]

> *Remember those who rule over (lead) you, who have spoke the word of God to you, whose faith follow, considering the outcome of their conduct. Jesus Christ is the same yesterday, today, and forever.*
> Hebrews 13:7-8

Act III: The Great Escape

Chapter 30: Please Note the Nearest Exit

Now that you're well aware of the damage that porn can cause, it's time to focus on what you need to do to break free from this addiction. I'm assuming that since you're still reading, you're serious about seeing this thing through. I've got to warn you, the road ahead is going to be long and difficult. There will be times when you'll want to give up. You may even stumble. This isn't for the faint of heart. However, you can do all things through Christ who strengthens you (Phil 4:13). If you fall, pick yourself up *quickly*, dust yourself off, and get right back on track. The enemy is hoping that you get frustrated and give up, but he's a defeated foe and we're not going to give him the satisfaction, right? Make sure your seat belts are on and your tray tables are locked into the upright position. We're preparing for takeoff.

Chapter 31: Repentance

The first step of this process is to achieve spiritual equilibrium. You need some balance. As of right now, you're way off kilter. Your life is like a see-saw with Sally Struthers on one side and one of the starving children she represents on the other. In order to achieve equilibrium, you need to start with repentance. The process of repentance involves two steps – both are of equal importance. First, you need to ask God's forgiveness. The Bible says in 1 John 1:9 that if we confess our sins, He is faithful and just to forgive us our sins and cleanse us from all unrighteousness. Confessing your sins is an admission of guilt. You're exposing yourself to your heavenly Father (even though He can already see everything). This step is very humbling. He already knows what you've done before your confession, so you'd have to assume that the process is necessary for more than just exposure. After all, you've already been exposed. This process is imperative, because it shows the condition of your heart. Asking for forgiveness puts things in perspective. When you fall into a lifestyle of habitual sin, your priorities shift, so all you care about is yourself. The act of repentance brings equilibrium to your priorities, so you're able to see clearly that your will, your plans, and your priorities do not trump those of God. The process makes it ever-so-clear that you are nothing without Him.

The second and equally important part of repentance involves turning away from our sin. If you ask for forgiveness just to make yourself feel better but don't take the necessary steps to walk away from your sin, your repentance isn't true, even if your confession was sincere. I know the story all too well. During the peak of my addiction, I tried to avoid church at all costs. If you're involved in habitual sin, you're not going to be comfortable attending church (assuming your pastor addresses the issues). So you have a couple of options. You can address the elephant in the room and work towards recovery; you can find another church; or you could just attend so infrequently that the conviction presented wasn't nearly as affective. I chose the latter.

I had a pattern. When I knew I was going to church, I would often get up early, watch porn and masturbate before getting ready. Before I left the house, I would completely delete my porn stash. I never kept magazines or hard copies of porn. That was too permanent for me. Rather, I kept digital movies on my computer. It made it easier to get rid of whenever I was feeling guilty and wanted to "repent." Then, I would go to church, cry out to God, ask for forgiveness, and then assume everything would be fixed.   Shortly after church was over, I'd find myself back in my room, door closed, looking for more illicit material with which to pollute my soul.   Though I would sincerely ask for forgiveness while in church, my repentance was never genuine, because I didn't take the necessary steps to truly turn and walk away from my sins. We'll further discuss the steps you'll need to take a little later, but it's important to know that in order to reap the benefits of freedom, you're going to have to change – change your lifestyle, change your habits, and change your heart. That is true repentance.

Chapter 32: Forgiveness

Having God forgive you is only part of the equation. You also need to learn how to forgive yourself. For most people this can be difficult, but for someone with years and years of deviant sexual behavior, this can prove to be a more serious challenge. Even though I knew God had forgiven me, I had a really hard time accepting His forgiveness and forgiving myself. As stated before, the enemy is the accuser of the brethren. When you attempt to break free from his chains he has a tendency to bombard you with guilt. He wants you to look back at who you were instead of looking ahead to who you can be. As Andy Dufresne said in *The Shawshank Redemption*, "Hope is a good thing, maybe the best of things, and no good thing ever dies." While I certainly agree with the first part, I know for a fact that the second part is off the mark. The entire purpose of the enemy's mission is to crush our hope and get us discouraged. If he can succeed in that, he has already won. When people are discouraged, often times they quit. He wants you to question your commitment, question God's forgiveness, and question your ability to change. When you start thinking things like "How can God forgive me for all of the things I've done?" and you begin to dwell on your sins instead of the Word of God, you're walking down a destructive path.

> *Therefore if anyone is in Christ, he is a new creation; old things have passed away; behold, all things have become new.*
>
> 2 Corinthians 5:17

This is an excellent scripture to commit to memory. After you've memorized it, you need to meditate on it day and night. The word *meditate* means to murmur. During your recovery, you need to audibly say this scripture every couple of minutes. You should be doing it at least a hundred times a day. I know it may sound excessive, but the repetition is necessary. You need to have a revelation as it relates to this issue and meditating on the Word of God is the only way. Until you recognize and truly understand that you are a new creation, you'll be stuck where you are. With the revelation that you're a new creation comes the hope of knowing that you are not who you used to be, and your past does not dictate your future. It took me about 6 weeks of meditating on this scripture before I got the revelation. It was as if something just clicked in my spirit and suddenly I got it. When it happened, I wept with joy. It was as if my record had been expunged. I finally realized that I didn't have to beat myself up anymore over the mistakes I made, because God wasn't holding me accountable for them. I was a new creation; that old man was dead and gone.

Chapter 33: Acceptance

One of the biggest reasons Christians struggle with this addiction for so long is because they're waiting on God. The problem is that God is waiting on you. He's not *going* to deliver you; He *already has* delivered you. Your debt has been paid. Your freedom has been purchased. You have a God-given right to experience freedom from this bondage, but you have to accept this gift of freedom. When Jesus died on the cross, He bore our sin, our sickness, and our disease. Whatever He died for, you were delivered from. This includes the bondage associated with addiction. Much like salvation, you cannot experience this gift unless you first accept it.

Accepting your deliverance is as easy as saying a prayer. You need to pray and acknowledge God. Let Him know that you believe His Word. Thank Him for setting you free. Then, ask for His wisdom and guidance as it relates to taking the necessary steps to continue to walk in this deliverance. Remember, "Faith without works is dead" (James 2:20). This scripture basically means that your actions should be the result of what you believe. Your words and your actions are a barometer of your faith. They expose what you believe – what you have faith for. If you truly believe the Word of God as it relates to your deliverance, then your words and your actions should reflect that. Saying things like, "I'll never beat this problem," or "Every time I try to abstain, it goes well for a while and then I stumble," are indications that you don't truly believe what you say you believe.

Now, does accepting your deliverance mean that everything will be peachy keen from that moment forward? Absolutely not. In fact, after you accept your deliverance, you probably aren't going to feel much different. Your spirit will be instantaneously changed, but it will take lots of hard work and discipline to get your flesh to fall in line.

Chapter 34: Identification

It has been said that if you knew better, you would do better. Many people think they know something, but don't really understand. People who smoke know that continuing to smoke dramatically increases their chance of getting lung cancer, and yet they still smoke. They may know that cigarettes cause cancer, but they don't truly understand. If they did, they wouldn't do it. When I was a child, I watched my grandmother lay in a hospital bed suffering for months on end, dying of lung cancer. She had many opportunities to quit smoking while there was still time to make a difference. When her cancer was first detected, it was manageable and the doctors were confident that they she would make a full recovery *if she stopped smoking*. The problem is she didn't. She knew, but she didn't understand, and she paid the ultimate price for her lack of understanding.

Knowing and truly understanding our own identity is critical to the success of our Christian walk. Many Christians don't know or understand who they are in Christ and what that entails. They're ignorant of the authority God has bestowed upon us, and as a result their lives are lacking. There's nothing that the enemy loves more than an ignorant Christian. As I previously mentioned, we have a role in righteousness. Too many Christians are waiting for God to do something, while God is waiting for them to do something. Know this: God has already done all that He's going to do. *Selah.* When Jesus said, "It is finished," and hung his head to die, He meant that the Trinity's role has been fulfilled. Finished. Done. Complete. When the Holy Spirit came to dwell within man, that was the icing on the cake. At that point, Christians were given all authority AND power in heaven, on earth, and under the earth.

For people coming from denominational backgrounds, this may be an unfamiliar concept. Many denominations teach us that we are to fully rely on God. While the idea sounds pious and Biblical, it's quite the opposite. Yes, we are to rely on God as our source. He is the creator of all, the beginning and the end. However, that does not alleviate us of our own responsibility, and the biggest problem is that many Christians think it does. To the average Christian, the idea of fully relying on God means sitting around waiting on Him to do something. The Bible, however, teaches us that He is the source of power, but we are the instruments He uses to get things done. It's a partnership. We have a covenant with Him.

Because of the fall of man, dominion of this world was given to Satan. Originally, it was given to mankind via Adam, but because of man's sin the keys to the castle were handed over to the devil. Now, because of God's law, He needs a willing participant to be able to act on the earth. Think about it. God knew the plan from the beginning. He knew that the first Adam would fall, so He always planned to have the last Adam (Jesus) come to deliver us. When evil had begun to take over the earth and Jesus' lineage was in danger of being wiped out, He summoned Noah to build an Ark (Genesis 6). God could not flood the earth to wipe out the evil without the willing participation of a man because complete and total destruction of the earth would contradict the plan that He set in motion. God even asked Mary's permission to use her as a vehicle to bring His son into the world.

We all know that God is omnipotent. He is all-powerful. However, His all-powerful nature does not come without limitations. For example, He cannot contradict His own Word. God's Word is what created the universe. The sun, moon, stars and planets are all hung by His command. If He were to ever go back on His Word, it would render His Word obsolete. If that were the case, the world that we live in would cease to exist because the power holding it in place would've been nullified. The Bible says, "God is not a man that He should lie, nor the son of man that He should change His mind" (Numbers 23:19 NIV).

This brings us to the main point of this section: What does God say about you? Who does He say that you are? Ultimately, His opinion is the only one that matters, even more so than your own. He is your Creator. He specifically created you with a purpose and destiny in mind; therefore, He is the only one who can tell you who you are. So, what does He say about you?

> *For I know the thoughts that I think toward you, says the Lord, thoughts of peace and not of evil, to give you a future and a hope. Then you will call upon Me and go and pray to Me, and I will listen to you. And you will seek Me and find Me, when you search for Me with all your heart. I will be found by you, says the Lord, **and I will bring you back from your captivity.***
> Jeremiah 27:11-14a

But you are a chosen generation, a royal priesthood, a holy nation, His own special people, that you may proclaim the praises of Him who called you out of darkness into His marvelous light; who once were not a people but are now the people of God, who had not obtained mercy by now have obtained mercy.
1 Peter 2:9-10

God has said some pretty impressive things about you. He doesn't think you're a loser or a failure. He created you to be victorious. He created us in His likeness. But what does that mean, exactly? Does it mean that physically we look like Him? Does God have two eyes, two ears, a nose, and a mouth? Does He have two arms, two legs, two hands, two feet, ten fingers and toes? God is a spirit. He doesn't have a physical body; therefore, being made in His image must mean something more substantial than the superficiality of our physical bodies. We've already established that we are triune beings in the same manner that God is, but our similarities don't end there. God is a speaking spirit. He decrees things, and they come to pass. Read the first chapter of Genesis if you don't believe me. How many times does the phrase "Then (or and) God said..." appear?

He said, and said, and said, and said. Every time He spoke, His authority set things into motion. By the end of the chapter it says, "Then God *saw* everything that He had made, and indeed it was very good." This is very important. It is imperative that you understand this. When God breathed the breath of life into mankind through Adam, that gift was given to us. The breath of life came with the ability to speak life.

Death and life are in the power of the tongue, and those who love it will eat its fruit.
Proverbs 18:21

Keep your heart with all diligence, for out of it spring the issues of life.
Proverbs 4:23

Either make the tree good and its fruit good, or else make the tree bad and its fruit bad; for a tree is known by its fruit. Brood of vipers! How can you, being evil,

speak good things? **For out of the abundance of the heart the mouth speaks.** *A good man out of the good treasure of his heart brings forth good things, and an evil man out of the evil treasure brings forth evil things. But I say to you that for every idle word men may speak, they will give account of it in the day of judgment. For by your words you will be justified, and by your words you will be condemned.*
Matthew 12:33-37

These three scriptures are connected and are directly related to your identity. The Bible says that God calls those things which be not as though they were (Romans 4:17). He spoke things into existence. Because you are made in God's image, you share this ability. According to Proverbs 18:21, this ability can either be a blessing or a curse. It all depends on what's coming out of your mouth; and since what's coming out of your mouth is the result of what's in your heart, it's extremely important to guard what's getting into your heart. Does that make sense? Later on, we'll go into more detail about how to guard your heart, but for now I just need you to grasp the importance of your words. Whether you like it or not, your words have power. Therefore, you should never speak anything that is contrary to the Word of God or contrary to what you want. In addition, you should take every opportunity you can to speak life and decree the blessings of God. Use your words to set blessings into action so that they can translate from the spiritual realm and manifest themselves into the physical.

As it relates to spiritual warfare, the Word of God is our sword. When spoken with conviction and authority, that Word is sharper than any double-edge sword. When the enemy tries to tempt you, you have the authority and the ability to speak to that temptation. Look at Jesus, our example. When He was tempted, what did he do? He spoke. He spoke the Word of God.

So many people speak death and destruction into their lives. When fear is in their heart, it comes out through their mouths. I had a coworker a while back who was constantly talking negative about her life and her situation, and it seemed the more she spoke, the more negative things seem to pile on top of her. I remember her saying things like "Every time I get some money, something bad happens," or "My roommate is sick, so I'll probably get sick soon." Without failure, everything she spoke managed to manifest itself in her life. So I ask you, what kinds of things are coming out of your mouth?

So, we know who God is, and we know who we are, but who is the enemy? We know him as Lucifer, Satan, and the devil to name a few. He is the antagonist in this story. When he was created, Lucifer was God's most brilliant creation. He was far more beautiful than any other angel. Unfortunately, Lucifer thought so too. In fact, he let his pride carry him away. He saw the angels worshipping God and thought that he too should be worshipped. His fantasy ended abruptly as God accosted him and hurled him down to earth. The Bible says that he fell to earth from heaven like lightning (Luke 10:18). Picking yourself up off of the ground after being cast out of heaven must be a sobering reality. Fast forward a bit (probably millions of years, since I tend to believe the Gap Theory aka the Ruin-Reconstruction Theory) and you have the creation of man. Suddenly, Lucifer isn't the greatest thing God created. His embarrassment and humiliation is replaced by jealousy and rage. He was once the apple of God's eye, but that role has been given to mankind. As beautiful as Lucifer was, he was not created in God's image. We were. Despite the fact that he was given free will, he was not given the opportunity for redemption. We were. Everything that he lacks was given to mankind, and that frustrates him to no end. In fact, since we were made in God's image, I'd be willing to bet that every time Satan looks at us, he is reminded of God. He sees the face of the one who casted him out of heaven, and his hatred for us grows. That's who Satan is, and that's precisely why he hates us. We remind him of his defeat. The Bible has already outlined the end of the story. We know that he is a defeated foe, but he is hell-bent (quite literally) on dragging down as many of us as he can. Now that you know who the enemy is, let's talk about how to exercise our authority over him.

Chapter 35: Detox

Wikipedia defines detox as "the physiological or medicinal removal of toxic substances from a living organism, including, but not limited to, the human body and additionally can refer to the period of withdrawal during which an organism returns to homeostasis after long-term use of an addictive substance." Read that definition again. Now, think about how that applies to drug and alcohol addictions. When people use drugs or alcohol to the point where they develop an addiction, the body begins to depend on those substances to function. This is in addition to the emotional and/or psychological dependency that is developed due to the enjoyment of their intoxication. It's a fascinating (not in a good way) thing to watch.

I used to work with a guy named Jim. After a while, he and I became pretty good friends. One day, I found out that he was an alcoholic. We were going to the mall to grab some lunch when he asked if we could run by his house for a minute. I didn't mind, so we swung by. I noticed in the car on the way that Jim was fidgety – like he had to pee really bad or had an itch that he couldn't scratch. When we entered his house, I saw a jug of vodka sitting on the coffee table next to an open bottle of club soda. He walked over to the table and poured himself a shot. That shot was followed by a swig of club soda. He repeated this routine several times (at least five) until the contents of the vodka bottle were completely depleted. After the last shot, he shook his head violently from side to side like a dog trying to dry himself off after a bath. "Alright, I'm good now," he said as he walked passed me and headed back to the car. I was amazed. Apparently, that was his sole reason for coming home. He needed a fix. Much to my surprise, he wasn't drunk, at all. He needed that to function. That was enough alcohol to put me down for a day, and I'm twice his size. I couldn't believe it. It made me look at him differently – part of it was a self-righteous, haughty look. I thought, "Man, how in the world do you get like that at 23 years old?" At the same time, I pitied him. I couldn't imagine what it was like to be that controlled by an addiction. I guess it's kind of ironic because this happened several years ago, before I met my wife. At the time, I was deep into my addiction with porn. I couldn't see it then, but my life shared many similarities with Jim's. Because I lived a couple of miles away from the office, I used to run home for "lunch" in the middle of the day. "Lunch" really meant that I was going home to watch porn and jerk off while my parents were at work, and I had the house to myself. I was controlled in the exact same way.

When I accepted the truth about my addiction, I realized that I had to go through detox, just like any other addict. I needed to purge my spirit of all of the filthy things I had grown addicted to over the years. I had to learn how to function without getting my fix. From a spiritual standpoint, the detox process begins with renewing your mind.

> *I beseech you therefore, brethren, by the mercies of God, that you present your bodies a living sacrifice, holy, acceptable to God, which is your reasonable service. And do not be conformed to this world, but be transformed by the renewing of your mind, that you may prove what is that good and acceptable and perfect will of God.*
> Romans 12:1-2

> *This I say, therefore, and testify in the Lord, that you should no longer walk as the rest of the Gentiles walk, in the futility of their mind, having their understanding darkened, being alienated from the life of God, because of the ignorance that is in them, because of the blindness of their heart; who, being past feeling, have given themselves over to lewdness, to work all uncleanness with greediness. But you have not so learned Christ, if indeed you have heard Him and have been taught by Him, as the truth is in Jesus: that you put off, concerning your former conduct, the old man which grows corrupt according to the deceitful lusts, and be renewed in the spirit of your mind, and that you put on the new man which was created according to God, in true righteousness and holiness.*
> Ephesians 4:17-24

Although the spiritual transformation that happens when you accept Jesus as your Lord and Savior or ask God to forgive your sins is instantaneous, the process of renewing one's mind is gradual and tedious – I know I sound like a broken record, but it is absolutely imperative that you grasp this concept. You'll learn as you go along that sexual purity is so much more than just not watching porn. Though it may be the biggest and most obvious problem, during this process you'll see that the dilemma does in fact go deeper than that. The problem is that your flesh has corrupted your soul (your mind, your will, your emotions) and the habitual use of porn exacerbates the problem. Unfortunately, simply removing the porn from the equation doesn't cure you. Don't get me wrong, it's part of the healing process, but the removal process in and of itself will not make you whole. Look at it this way: imagine that your porn addiction is like a termite infestation of your property. I've worked in pest control, so I'm quite familiar with how termites operate. Subterranean termites live underground and often penetrate your home through small cracks in the foundation. Most of the time, these types of infestations go undetected for quite some time. However, by the time you recognize that there's a problem, tremendous damage may have already been done to your home. Termites eat the cellulose material in your home, mainly the wood. They'll eat through floor joists, support beams, and hardwood floors. Even if you get a treatment done that kills the termites attacking the house, your relief will be short-lived if you don't eliminate the entire colony. Furthermore, simply killing off all of the termites eating the house doesn't restore the house back to its original condition. The structural integrity of the house has already been compromised and needs to be restored. If all of the old, damaged wood that the termites were feasting on is not removed and replaced along with destroying the termite shelter tubes, the likelihood of an infestation in the future is pretty high. Here's why: termites are blind, and they travel based on instinct. Everywhere they go, they leave a pheromone trail, so they can find their way back. Once they've identified a food source, they leave their scent, so all of the other termites can find the location. If that wood is not removed, it will continue to lure other termites. The curative solution is two fold. First, you must put a protective barrier around the property – a colony elimination toxin. Then, you must remove and restore the areas of the house that have been damaged.

Now, think about what I just said and apply that to a lustful lifestyle and porn addiction. The house is your soul and lust (porn more specifically) is the termites. Removal without restoration is work done in vain. The damage that porn does to you doesn't heal itself, just like your house will not heal itself. The curative process is very similar as well. You must put a barrier around yourself as well as remove and restore the damaged areas. Stay tuned, and we'll get into that shortly.

When you decide that you're going to make a change, the first 40 days are the toughest. Depending on how strong your addiction is, you may show physical signs of withdrawal as I did. These may include, but are not limited to headaches, nausea, chills, cold sweats, hives, and overall irritability. It is imperative that during these times you stand firm to your convictions, because it's not going to be easy. There were many times where I thought about quitting. There were times where I physically cried, because I missed porn so much. The thought of living the rest of my life without porn seemed like an impossible task, so like any recovering addict, I decided to take one day at a time. By being diligent and holding fast to my convictions, a day turned into a week, and week turned into a month, a month turned into a year and so on.

Chapter 36: Fasting

Fasting is a vital part of the detoxification process. It's also a practice that should be implemented on a regular basis for all Christians. The generic definition of fasting is the act of refraining for physical sustenance. However, there are other things a person can fast from in order to achieve positive results. You can fast from TV, movies, video games, sex, or pretty much anything that brings you pleasure.

Recently, my wife and I decided to fast from all social media outlets. I didn't realize how plugged in I was until those plugs were pulled. It was a sobering reality. I recommend occasional (or even regular) fasts from anything that has the potential to be addictive enough for you to exalt as an idol in your life.

The purpose of fasting is to bring things into perspective, as well as, bringing your flesh into subjection. Remember that we are triune beings. By physically starving our flesh, we are making it weaker, while increasing the receptiveness of our spirits. We enjoy a heightened sensitivity to the voice of God via Holy Spirit when we are in the midst of fasting. This is critical because too many Christians spend too much time talking to God and don't spend enough time listening. God is like a radio station; He is always broadcasting. The problem is that we often have our radios off and miss the message. When we miss the mark, it's not because God wasn't speaking to us. It's because we weren't listening. Fasting helps to put an end to that.

There are, however, some things to keep in mind while fasting. Fasting for the sake of fasting can be ineffective if your heart isn't in the right place. There have been times in the past where the church I was attending at the time had planned a corporate fast, and while I participated because the pastor told me to, my heart was in the wrong place. I did it out of obligation and didn't spend any time in God's presence. Needless to say, that time didn't really produce positive results. To obtain the best results from fasting, one needs to spend ample time in the Word and in God's presence. Fasting breaks down the flesh, while spending time in God's presence builds up our spirits. Each practice by itself can produce positive results; however, combining the two is the best way to get the best outcome. The fast creates a window of opportunity for growth, faith, and revelation that may not have otherwise been possible.

*And when they had come to the multitude, a man came
to Him, kneeling down to Him and saying, "Lord, have
mercy on my son, for he is an epileptic and suffers
severely; for he often falls into the fire and often into the
water. So I brought him to Your disciples, but they could
not cure him." Then Jesus answered and said, "O
faithless and perverse generation, how long shall I be
with you? How long shall I bear with you? Bring him
here to Me." And Jesus rebuked the demon, and it came
out of him; and the child was cured from that very hour.
Then the disciples came to Jesus privately and said,
"Why could we not cast it out?" So Jesus said to them,
"Because of your unbelief; for assuredly, I say to you, if
you have faith as a mustard seed, you will say to this
mountain, 'Move from here to there,' and it will move;
and nothing will be impossible for you. However, this
kind does not go out except by prayer and fasting."*
Matthew 17:14-21

I believe that this verse has been interpreted incorrectly by many
people. I think that most people walk away from this verse thinking that
there are certain kinds of demons that can only be cast out with prayer
and fasting. In my opinion this is the wrong interpretation of this verse.
Consider this: the Bible says that the name of Jesus is above every name.
It also says that every knee shall bow and every tongue shall confess that
Jesus is Lord. Now, if this verse is implying that you must first pray and
fast in order to cast out a demon, then this verse is essentially saying that
the name of Jesus and the authority thereof is not sufficient enough to do
the job, which in turn would be a contradiction of God's word, right?

I believe that when Jesus said "However, this kind does not go
out except by prayer and fasting," He was talking about their unbelief.
Remember earlier in the verse when they asked him why they couldn't
cast it out, He said because of their unbelief. Unbelief is a characteristic
of a lack of faith, and it's one of the conditions in our lives that can cause
our God-given authority to be ineffective. It's not that the name of Jesus
isn't powerful and effective; it's that your faith needs a shot in the arm.
How many times did Jesus say to His disciples "O ye of little faith"?
Their lack of faith was a constant struggle and He was showing them
that:

a.) their level of effectiveness directly correlates with their level of faith and

b.) there are steps that they could take to increase and strengthen their faith. Fasting is one of those steps.

From a physical standpoint, fasting acts as somewhat of a distraction to your flesh. When you're detoxifying your flesh and renewing your mind, it can be challenging. Your flesh is used to having its way, especially as it relates to lust. These lustful cravings can be intense and often downright painful. It's like a screaming child that is dying for some attention. When you fast from eating food, hunger then becomes your most noticeable desire. This is not to say that your flesh doesn't still crave the lustful attention you've been feeding it, because it does. However, your physical hunger tends to take precedence. This gives you ample opportunity to focus on what you're fasting for. Your hunger is a constant reminder of what you're trying to accomplish. When I fast, I honor God with my lips every time I feel a hunger pain or think about eating. It's my way of staying focused. Oftentimes I'll quote Matthew 4:4 which says, "Man does not live by bread alone, but by every word that proceeds from the mouth of God." This is what Jesus said to Satan when Satan tried to tempt Him with food during a long fast. Heck, the way I see it, if it's good enough for Jesus, it's good enough for me.

At the beginning of your journey, I recommend fasting from food for 1-2 days. I also recommend fasting from all distracting, technological outlets like TV, the internet, video games, Facebook, etc for at least a week. This provides ample time for fellowship with your Father without distractions. If you could plan this time around an outdoor excursion like a camping trip, it would be ideal. Nothing seems to bring you close to God's presence than surrounding yourself with His creations out in nature.

If you're married and have been struggling with porn, I recommend fasting from all forms of physical intimacy with your wife for at least a week. This also means no masturbation. Your priorities need to be reset and aligned properly. Your viewing porn says that you don't appreciate your wife and you need to rekindle that longing for her and her alone. Loss is the quickest cure for ingratitude, and nothing will make you appreciate sex more than giving it up for a while. The Apostle Paul laid the groundwork for permitting abstinence during a time of fasting in his first letter to the Corinthians.

Now concerning the things of which you wrote to me: It is good for a man not to touch a woman. Nevertheless, because of sexual immorality, let each man have his own wife, and let each woman have her own husband. Let the husband render to his wife the affection due her, and likewise also the wife to her husband. The wife does not have authority over her own body, but the husband does. And likewise the husband does not have authority over his own body, but the wife does. ***Do not deprive one another except with consent for a time, that you may give yourselves to fasting and prayer; and come together again so that Satan does not tempt you because of your lack of self-control.*** *But I say this as a concession, not as a commandment. For I wish that all men were even as I myself. But each one has his own gift from God, one in this manner and another in that. But I say to the unmarried and to the widows: It is good for them if they remain even as I am; but if they cannot exercise self-control, let them marry. For it is better to marry than to burn with passion.*

1 Corinthians 7:1-9

Chapter 37: Idle Hands are the Devil's Workshop

One of the more difficult things you're going to have to do during this process is find creative and productive ways to occupy your time. If you're like me and spent several hours a day watching porn, you'll find yourself with tons and tons of free time on your hands. When I first started this journey, I avoided the internet altogether. Because the majority of my time online consisted of my watching porn I found that staying offline, at least in the beginning, was the best and most effective way to prevent myself from falling back into old habits.

You also want to make sure that what you're filling this time with isn't something detrimental. The last thing you need is transfer addiction where you bounce from one vice to the other. Again, this is the perfect opportunity to fellowship with God and learn more about Him. Spending time in prayer and in the Word is always helpful. You also might want to take up journaling. I spent my time writing this book and putting these principles into practice.

Chapter 38: Baptism of the Holy Spirit

I don't want to make the mistake of assuming that all of my audience knows and understand the baptism of the Holy Spirit, so this section is going to be a bit of a theology lesson. Holy Spirit is the helper and comforter that Jesus promised us before He ascended back to heaven. It is the third part of God's triune nature. Baptism of the Holy Spirit is also referred to as being filled with the Spirit. Contrary to popular opinion, this is a separate experience from being born of the spirit. When a person accepts Jesus Christ as his savior, he is born of the spirit. This means that his spirit has been reborn into God's family. Being filled with Holy Spirit is something completely different. There are plenty of Christians who accept Jesus as their Lord and Savior and never experience the power that comes with the indwelling of the Holy Spirit. This does not affect their salvation. When they die, they will most certainly go to heaven and spend eternity with Christ. It does, however, limit their ability and effectiveness here on earth.

When referring to the power of Holy Spirit in the New Testament, there are two Greek words that are used – dunamis and exousia. Exousia is defined as our authority or our right to act, while dunamis is our power and our ability to get the job done. Think about a police officer. His badge gives him authority to do what he does. His gun gives the power to carry out his authority, should you choose not to honor the badge. In the movie *Righteous Kill*, Robert De Niro plays an over-zealous cop who is being investigated for alleged vigilante justice. He has a great quote in the movie that I think is applicable here. He said, "Most people respect the badge. Everybody respects the gun." In our society, there are law-abiding citizens who would respect the authority of the police whether they carried guns or not. I fall into that category. I'm not a criminal, and I've got nothing to hide. If a police officer tells me to do something, I'm going to do it. There are, however, factions in society (many of whom are criminals) who would not respect the authority of the police officers if the threat of violence and power was not present in the form of the officer's gun.

During the Great Commission, Jesus told us that all authority in heaven and on earth had been given to Him (Matthew 28:18). By accepting Him as our Savior, we now have the right to operate under that same authority. This is exousia.

*But you shall receive **power** when the Holy Spirit has come upon you; and you shall be witnesses to Me in Jerusalem, and in all Judea and Samaria, and to the end of the earth.*

Acts 1:8

The power referred to in this scripture is dunamis. Holy Spirit gives us the power to exercise our authority when necessary. This is important because the devil and his minions are like the criminals who don't respect a police officer's authority alone. You have to demonstrate your power to force them into compliance. The enemy knows that if you're not filled with the Holy Spirit, you don't have the power on your own to bind him and cast him out. If a police officer stumbles upon an armed robbery in progress, how effective would he be if he didn't have a gun? Now, he can certainly get on the horn and radio for backup, but if he himself doesn't have a gun, he's probably not going to be able to stop the criminals from taking what they want. In that same respect, without power it's going to be difficult, if not impossible for you to stop the enemy. He comes to steal, kill, and destroy – none of which he has the right or the authority to do (because Christ took back that authority when He died and rose again), but if you don't have the power to force compliance, he's going to keep messing up things in your life until you stop him.

What if the devil gave your child leukemia? Without the power of Holy Spirit, you will be unable to exercise your authority to heal that child. One of the names for God is Jehovah Rapha which literally means, "I am the God who heals you." It is not God's desire that any of us should suffer through sickness or disease. He wants us to walk in divine health. He doesn't want our lives to be cut short because of the enemy, but He allows it to happen because He has to. When Adam sinned, authority of this world was given to Satan. When Jesus died and rose from the dead, that authority was taken back. However, we have to exercise that authority in order for it to manifest the results that we want. When you've exercised your authority and seen it manifest results, it builds your faith and your confidence. I saw my cousin healed of leukemia because of his mother's faith. With God, all things are possible and being filled with the Holy Spirit is the first step to living a miraculous life.

In order to be filled with the Spirit, you must first have been born of the spirit. After that, all you need to do is ask God. It's that simple. When you are filled with Holy Spirit, the evidence of this occurrence is speaking in tongues. When you look at the scriptural examples, every time someone was filled with the Holy Spirit, they spoke in tongues. The vast majority of the examples explicitly say this. In other examples, it's implied by saying something like "and when they saw that they had been filled….." You can't see the Holy Spirit, so the only way they could've seen that someone was filled was by the evidence of speaking in tongues.

Chapter 39: Praying in the Spirit

This section is really going to test your denominational roots. Unfortunately, many denominations teach and many Christians believe that praying in the spirit (also commonly referred to as speaking in tongues) is a practice that is no longer applicable to the modern-day church. I believe this is a shame and one of the greatest lies the devil ever got some people to believe. Many "moderate" Christians view speaking in tongues as something weird, strange, and even spooky. The truth is people fear what they don't understand.

Satan is many things, but you can never accuse him of being stupid. He's the ultimate strategist. Like an NFL head coach trying to outmaneuver his opponent by creating a game plan specifically for them, the devil has specific and effective strategies to try and overcome the body of Christ, both as a whole and us as individuals. So, if the devil has spent the last 2000 years trying to discredit praying in the spirit by making us believe that it's strange and weird, we have to ask ourselves why. If he doesn't want us to do it, there must be a reason – a benefit to us that is extremely detrimental to him and his agenda. And here it is: praying in the spirit makes you dangerous to him – plain and simple. This is warfare. We are at war with the enemy and his kingdom.

> *Finally, my brethren, be strong in the Lord and in the power of His might. Put on the whole armor of God, that you may be able to stand against the wiles of the devil. For we do not wrestle against flesh and blood, but against principalities, against powers, against the rulers of the darkness of this age, against spiritual hosts of wickedness in the heavenly places. Therefore take up the whole armor of God, that you may be able to withstand in the evil day, and having done all, to stand. Stand therefore, having girded your waist with truth, having put on the breastplate of righteousness, and having shod your feet with the preparation of the gospel of peace; above all, taking the shield of faith with which you will be able to quench all the fiery darts of the wicked one. And take the helmet of salvation, and the sword of the Spirit, which is the word of God; praying always with all prayer and supplication in the Spirit, being watchful to this end with all perseverance and supplication for all*

the saints— and for me, that utterance may be given to
me, that I may open my mouth boldly to make known the
mystery of the gospel, for which I am an ambassador in
chains; that in it I may speak boldly, as I ought to speak.
Ephesians 6:10-20

God is our Commander-in-Chief; Jesus is our Secretary of Defense; and Holy Spirit is our field General. God communicates to us through Holy Spirit, but we as the troops on the ground have the ability to communicate back to God through the same channel, by praying in the spirit. When we speak in tongues, the Holy Spirit is praying through us the perfect will of God. This is a communication line that Satan cannot tap. When we pray in the natural, the enemy hears us. He knows what we're requesting. He knows what we need. He knows our fears. He knows our struggles. How effective can your opponent be if he knows everything about you? It's hard to beat a team when they know what play you're about to run before you run it. Of course, the exception is the Packers during Lombardi's tenure as head coach. But for everyone else, part of being successful is being able to keep your opponent guessing. Satan cannot read your mind. The only way he knows what you're thinking is based on what you say and what you do. If you notice an attractive woman and the enemy whispers, "You know you want her." He doesn't know if that thought has taken root until you respond. If you continue to check her out, starring at her curves and longing for her, he knows you've taken the bait. If you bounce your eyes away immediately and rebuke that thought, he knows that you're resisting. When you pray in the spirit, he has absolutely no idea what you're praying about. He's left in the dark. In the same manner that we don't know what we're saying, he doesn't know either. This leaves him at a disadvantage.

Likewise the Spirit also helps in our weaknesses. For we
do not know what we should pray for as we ought, but
the Spirit Himself makes intercession for us with
groanings which cannot be uttered.
Romans 8:26

It pays to be sensitive to Holy Spirit. Have you ever been in a situation where you felt the urge to pray but didn't know what or who to pray for? This is when praying in the Spirit is most helpful. There are people and situations that need our prayer, but they may be unknown to us at the time. By praying in the Spirit, we allow Holy Spirit to pray through us the perfect will of God. There have been times in my life where my mom or dad will call me and say they felt the strong urge to pray for me last week and asked if something was going on. Every time this has happened, there was something major going on that day that they didn't know about, either the enemy was trying to attack my thoughts, or I was fighting off sickness or something. Their obedience ultimately helped me overcome whatever challenge I was facing at that point in time.

Praying in the Spirit also helps to strengthen our spirits. The Bible says that he who speaks in tongues edifies himself (1 Corinthians 14:4). The word *edify* means to strengthen or build up. We know Paul isn't talking about building up and strengthening our physical man. I can't bench press more weight just because I pray in the Spirit, so we have to assume that he's referring to our spirits. Praying in the Spirit makes our spirit man stronger, which is an important part of resisting temptation. As we talked about earlier, if our flesh is stronger than our spirit, we will fall into temptation much more often than we resist it. Having a strong spirit man means that we'll be able to withstand temptation and force our flesh to comply with the Word of God.

There are certain Christians who believe that while praying in the spirit is applicable to our modern-day church, it's a gift only available to some people, like the gift of prophecy. I want to address those people.

> *Now concerning spiritual gifts, brethren, I do not want you to be ignorant: You know that you were Gentiles, carried away to these dumb idols, however you were led. Therefore I make known to you that no one speaking by the Spirit of God calls Jesus accursed, and no one can say that Jesus is Lord except by the Holy Spirit. There are diversities of gifts, but the same Spirit. There are differences of ministries, but the same Lord. And there are diversities of activities, but it is the same God who works all in all. But the manifestation of the Spirit is given to each one for the profit of all: for to one is given the word of wisdom through the Spirit, to another the word of knowledge through the same Spirit, to another*

*faith by the same Spirit, to another gifts of healings by
the same Spirit, to another the working of miracles, to
another prophecy, to another discerning of spirits, to
another different kinds of tongues, to another the
interpretation of tongues. But one and the same Spirit
works all these things, distributing to each one
individually as He wills.*

1 Corinthians 12:1-11

There are those who believe that this scripture implies that
praying in the spirit isn't for all people. They believe it's a gift that some
people have and others don't. I disagree with that notion. Being filled
with Holy Spirit is the foundation for doing the miraculous. I don't
believe I have the gift of healing, but I won't hesitate to lay hands on
someone and command them to be healed. Why? Because God says I
have the authority to do it. There are those in ministry who have specific
gifts all the time, but I believe that Holy Spirit will empower a person
with a particular gift for the benefit of many. Consider this: the Bible
says a number of times that God is no respecter of persons and that there
is no partiality with God. This means that if God has done something for
one person, He will do it for everyone else, all things being equal. Now,
this doesn't mean that because he blessed your friend with a wife that
he'll bless you with one right now. Maybe you need to shower. Maybe
you need to shave. Maybe you need to lose weight and make yourself
more appealing. Maybe you need to work on you. Again, all things
being equal, God doesn't play favorites. The Bible specifically says that
praying in the spirit makes you stronger, so why would God give that gift
to some and not all? Why would he allow me to pray in the Spirit to
make my spirit man stronger and not offer you the exact same benefit?
That answer is: He wouldn't. That means, this gift has to be available to
ALL Christians who believe.

Speaking in tongues can be done both privately and publicly.
When it's done in private, there are very few rules or guidelines. I pray
in the Spirit every day. In fact, I pray in the Spirit more than I pray in the
natural. Overall, I just think it's more effective because I'm praying the
perfect will of God, and it's not limited to my own memory or
circumstances. When publicly praying in the Spirit, in a church setting,
there are a couple of things that need to be established. First, this has to
be done under the authority and with the permission of the pastor. I've

been in churches where certain individuals broke out into speaking in tongues at inappropriate times where it actually disrupted the service. I don't think this is God's intention. Speaking in tongues privately is about edifying you as an individual. Speaking in tongues publicly is about edifying the church through prophecy. Therefore, when speaking in tongues in a church setting, the ultimate goal is to hear a Word from God through prophecy.

> *How is it then, brethren? Whenever you come together, each of you has a psalm, has a teaching, has a tongue, has a revelation, has an interpretation. Let all things be done for edification. If anyone speaks in a tongue, let there be two or at the most three, each in turn, and let one interpret. But if there is no interpreter, let him keep silent in church, and let him speak to himself and to God. Let two or three prophets speak, and let the others judge. But if anything is revealed to another who sits by, let the first keep silent. For you can all prophesy one by one, that all may learn and all may be encouraged. And the spirits of the prophets are subject to the prophets. For God is not the author of confusion but of peace, as in all the churches of the saints. Let your women keep silent in the churches, for they are not permitted to speak; but they are to be submissive, as the law also says. And if they want to learn something, let them ask their own husbands at home; for it is shameful for women to speak in church. Or did the word of God come originally from you? Or was it you only that it reached? If anyone thinks himself to be a prophet or spiritual, let him acknowledge that the things which I write to you are the commandments of the Lord. But if anyone is ignorant, let him be ignorant. Therefore, brethren, desire earnestly to prophesy, and do not forbid to speak with tongues.* ***Let all things be done decently and in order.***
> 1 Corinthians 14:26-40

I think the last verse of this chapter is the most important. Ultimately, God wants everything to be done decently and in order. People are in church to learn and to receive from God, and He doesn't want someone to be distracted during this important time. Also, I want to address the part about women being silent in church. I know it has nothing to do with this topic or this book in general, but because it's part of this scripture it needs to be addressed. There are things that you should know about the culture of that time. Women in that day were highlight uneducated. And because many in the church were converted Jews (like Paul himself), they maintained many Jewish traditions. For example, the men sat separately from the women during church. You'd have men on one side and women on the other with a center aisle separating the groups. If a woman didn't understand something that was being said, she would often shout across the church to her husband asking him to explain what was being said. As you can imagine, this was quite disruptive. For this reason, and this reason alone, Paul said that women should be silent in church and to ask their husbands at home if they had questions. I don't believe that this is applicable today as our culture has changed and women are more educated. Getting back to praying in the Spirit: for a more in-depth look at the topic, I would suggest reading Kenneth Hagin's pamphlet called *Why Tongues.* Despite its pocket-sized stature, this pamphlet describes the importance of praying in the Spirit better than anything I've ever read, aside from the Bible of course.

Chapter 40: Spiritual Growth

As we stated earlier, accepting Jesus Christ as your Savior means that you are born of the Spirit. Just like a newborn baby, your newborn spirit needs nutrition. It needs to be fed properly, so that it can grow and develop. The Bible makes references to spiritual milk and spiritual meat. This is in reference to a person's spiritual development. If you're a new Christian, your spirit can only handle and digest spiritual milk or the basics of Christianity. As you grow and develop, you can handle more substantial spiritual meals.

> *For though by this time you ought to be teachers, you need someone to teach you again the first principles of the oracles of God; and you have come to need milk and not solid food. For everyone who partakes only of milk is unskilled in the word of righteousness, for he is a babe. But solid food belongs to those who are of full age, that is, those who by reason of use have their senses exercised to discern both good and evil.*
> Hebrews 5:12-14

According to the scripture, people who consume only spiritual milk are "unskilled in the word of righteousness" because they are babies. So what exactly does that mean? Essentially it means that those who are babies in Christ are unskilled at living a righteous lifestyle. They have the passion. They have the desire. They just don't have the skills and the knowledge. There are people who accept Jesus as their Savior and continue to live sinful lifestyles until they grow in spiritual maturity. Spiritual growth allows a person to mature spiritually. It's how they develop. As the rest of the scripture says "But solid food belongs to those who are of full age, that is, those who by reason of use have their senses exercised to discern both good and evil." There are new Christians who don't know that premarital sex is a sin and may continue with that practice after accepting Christ. The same can be said about pornography. But, after the revelation has been made that these things aren't pleasing to God, your spiritual growth is dependent on your ability to rid your life of these kinds of sins.

Being part of a *good* church is important to your spiritual growth. You need to be part of a church that teaches about the gifts of the spirit, tithing, and spiritual development. One of the biggest problems I have about most denominations is that they leave certain parts and practices out. I've been to churches where I could sit through an hour-long sermon and not gain anything that would impact my life. That's a problem. God designed the five-fold ministry to develop His people. If you're not learning biblical principles in church that you can then turn around and apply to your life to improve your life, then you're probably in a church where milk is the only thing on the menu. However, in order to grow and develop properly, you need spiritual meat. In the scripture above, the author is admonishing the Hebrews for their lack of spiritual development. Notice how he says "For though by this time you ought to be teachers, you need someone to again teach you the oracles of God, and you have come to need milk not solid food." He's basically saying, "Look, you should be teaching this stuff by now as opposed to having it taught to you again, and while you're still drinking milk, you should be eating meat."

Spiritual growth does no occur naturally. It's an intentional process. This means that a person could remain a spiritual baby his entire time on earth. It's quite possible for someone to sit in a dead church every Sunday for the rest of his life and not receive enough spiritual sustenance to grow and mature. Conversely, it's possible for a person to grow at a rapid pace based on his own hunger. Look at the Apostle Paul. He went from being the chief persecutor of Christians to God's mouthpiece for most of the New Testament. That's quite a maturation process, wouldn't you say? In order for you to have success at overcoming a sexual addiction, you need to grow and mature spiritually, because your spirit is what's going to fight your flesh. If your spirit remains a baby, it won't have much of a chance to defeat your "big, bad flesh."

Chapter 41: See No Evil, Hear No Evil

A big part of controlling the desires of your flesh lies with what kind of stimuli you're allowing into your eye gate and ear gate. There's an easy cause an effect argument for watching porn and committing sexual sins. However, there are other forms of visual and audio stimuli that are not so easily linked to your sexual behavior. In a situation like this, it would be dangerous to overlook those influences. We all know the obvious sources that you need to avoid like porn videos and images. That's a given. In my opinion, it's definitely worth discussing the not-so-obvious sources of arousal. Remember when I talked about how my eyes were out of control and I was checking out virtually every woman I saw? As I previously stated, every sensual image that I soaked up was like a snapshot for my brain that was catalogued and filed into my subconscious. Over time, enough of those images cumulatively built up my arousal creating a strong desire for sexual fulfillment.

You need to remove all of the things in your life that have the possibility of causing physical and/or emotional arousal. You also need to remove the things that get your mind thinking or moving in that direction and that are completely contrary to the Word of God. This is especially true when it is of a sensual/sexual nature.

Like Job, you need to make a covenant with your eyes not to look lustfully on a woman (Job 31:1). In my opinion, this includes all forms and outlets. Unless you're a doctor and it's part of your job, I believe that the only nudity you should visually absorb is that of your wife. Even though it may not "technically" be porn, TV or movies that have nudity will stir up the desires of your flesh and get you to crave more. Before I go and see a rated R movie, I visit www.kids-in-mind.com or www.imdb.com to view the content advisory. Kids-in-Mind is great. They rate movies on a 1-10 scale based on sex/nudity, violence/gore, and language. 1 means minimal, 10 means abundant amounts. Also, they go a step further and give you specific details about everything. For example, a movie might be rated as a 7 for sex/nudity and one of the explanations will say "A man and a woman kiss, he grabs her clothed butt, and sex is implied but not shown." It may also say, "Several scenes take place in a strip club and women's bare breast, thighs and buttocks are explicitly seen." Generally speaking, if there's nudity, I won't see that movie. There is one exception, and only one. If upon reading the content advisory I discover that there is one instance of *brief* nudity as described by the site and there is adequate information about when it occurs during the movie, I sometimes make an exception. This allows me know ahead of time when it's coming so I can cover my eyes. Also, I'll only do this when my wife is with me for accountability. Keep in mind that everyone is different. You may not have enough self control to cover your eyes when you know it's coming, so being honest with yourself is imperative. Don't use my liberty as an excuse to put yourself in a situation where you're tempted.

Remember, everyone is different. My flesh may have different desire than yours, therefore causing me to protect myself differently than you do. For example, I love rhythmic dancing. To me there's nothing more exotic and arousing than a woman with rhythm. So, there are certain things that I have to avoid that may not be a problem for someone else. A perfect example is the show *Dancing with the Stars*. I do not and cannot watch that show. For me, a combination of ballroom dancing and skimpy outfits is a huge recipe for disaster, so I stay away altogether. For someone else, that may not be an issue. The key here is using wisdom and asking Holy Spirit for guidance.

The Bible says that all things work together for good for those who love the Lord and are called according to His purpose (Romans 8:28). Being aware of your triggers has its benefits. As I just mentioned, I find dancing very arousing. I'm aware of that, and so is my wife. My wife use to do an exercise program called Zumba which is a latin-based dancercise with lots of hip rolling and booty shaking. It's like one of Shakira's music videos. It's so sensual and erotic it's amazing. Now, I couldn't watch her classes or the instructional videos because it involves other women being sensual, but I was all about her giving me a private dance to show me what she had learned.

I used to watch this show called *Cheaters*. It's typical late-night, trash TV. If you're not familiar with the show, allow me to elaborate. Basically, a partner who thinks their significant other is cheating contacts the show. The show will then get private investigators to follow said people and gather footage to confirm the infidelity. After the evidence is presented to the person who called the show, the cheating partner is confronted on camera and the madness ensues. It is purely indulgent. It's like the Jerry Springer's and Soap Operas of the world. I used to watch that show religiously. I always thought it was hilarious watching the people getting busted. One night my wife asked me if that's really the kind of show that I should be watching. Immediately, I got defensive. I told her that there was no nudity and therefore shouldn't be a problem. She told me she didn't think that it was something that a Godly man should be feeding his spirit. Then she threw down her Ace in the hole. She asked me, "Would you watch that show with Dr. Mike?" Dr. Mike was referring to my [former] pastor Dr. Michael A. Freeman, who wrote the foreword for this book. After thinking about it briefly, I knew she had a point. I admitted that no, I probably wouldn't be watching that show with him, to which she replied, "If you wouldn't watch it with him, then you probably shouldn't be watching it at all." I knew she was right, and I haven't watched that show since. Sometimes Holy Spirit uses our wives to get His point across to us.

It's also worth mentioning that you should guard your ears from musical lyrics that get you thinking about sex. Though it's easy to blame rap and R&B as the prime culprits for sexualized music, there are things to avoid in all genres of music. Again, let Holy Spirit be your guide.

Chapter 42: The Power of Praise

Praise is what I do, even when I'm going through
I've learned to worship You
No my circumstance doesn't even stand a chance
My praise outweighs the bad
And I vow to praise You
Through the good and the bad
I'll praise You whether happy or sad
I'll praise You in all that I go through
Because praise is what I do
And I owe it all to You
William Murphy – Praise Is What I Do

A sad truth about the Body of Christ is the fact that too many Christian are trying to battle the enemy without using all of the weapons God has given us. To be successful against a formidable opponent, one must pull out all the stops and use every weapon in the arsenal. Did you know that the praise of a believer is a powerful weapon? When I was a kid, my dad used to tell me that praising God put lumps on the devil's head. He can't stand it when we praise and worship God. When we praise God, it not only affects the enemy, it affects God and us as well. The Bible says that God inhabits the praises of His people (Psalm 22:3). The word inhabit means to dwell or abide in. God lives within our praise. What does that mean for the enemy? Well, we know that Satan cannot stand the presence of God. Satan is a liar, and he is exposed for who and what he is in the presence of God. This means that if God is present, Satan is not. He can't be. Praising God in the midst of the storm brings His presence on the scene which subsequently forces the devil out.

There are two scriptures that I want to take a closer look at.

Out of the mouth of babes and nursing infants You have
ordained strength, because of Your enemies that You
may silence the enemy and the avenger.
Psalm 8:2

And Jesus said to them, "Yes. Have you never read,
'Out of the mouth of babes and nursing infants You
have perfected praise'?"

If you read these scriptures, you may initially get the impression that Jesus misquoted the verse in Psalm. Knowing that he is God in the flesh, the other alternative is to accept the idea that He is giving us more revelation as to what the scripture really means. The first scripture says "You have ordained strength," while the second says, "You have perfected praise." To me, this says that God is equating praise with strength. When we praise God, we are magnifying Him. This means we're making Him bigger – bigger than our problems, bigger than our circumstances, and bigger than anything this world can throw at us. Whatever you focus on will expand. *Selah.* As it relates to sin and temptation, when we focus on the temptation in front of us, it gets bigger. It's in our focus and we can't see any way around it. However, when we focus on God by praising Him in all of His glory, we begin to see and realize that He is bigger and more real to us than our problems are. Once, I heard someone say, "Stop telling God how big your problem is, and start telling your problem how big your God is." *Selah.*

Chapter 43: Unsheathe Your Sword

I believe that the best defense is a good offense. This is true in sports, and it's also true in spiritual warfare. The enemy is going to constantly test your resolve by throwing sensual thoughts your way. You can't change the fact that he's going to put thoughts in your head, but you are responsible for what you do with those thoughts. It's been said that you can't stop the birds from flying around your head, but you can stop them from making a nest in your hair. The Bible says that we are to bring every thought captive to the obedience of Christ.

> *Now I, Paul, myself am pleading with you by the meekness and gentleness of Christ—who in presence am lowly among you, but being absent am bold toward you. But I beg you that when I am present I may not be bold with that confidence by which I intend to be bold against some, who think of us as if we walked according to the flesh. For though we walk in the flesh, we do not war according to the flesh. For the weapons of our warfare are not carnal but mighty in God for pulling down strongholds, casting down arguments and every high thing that exalts itself against the knowledge of God, bringing every thought into captivity to the obedience of Christ, and being ready to punish all disobedience when your obedience is fulfilled.*
> 2 Corinthians 10:1-6

The Word of God is our sword as it relates to spiritual warfare. Look back at Jesus' example. When Satan tempted Him, He answered with the Word. He fought back. Satan can't stand it when believers speak the Word of God with authority. Whenever I'm in a situation where he tries to plant an impure thought in my head, I say "I rebuke that thought (or image) in the name of Jesus. I am a man of God and I reject, rebuke and cast down anything that is contrary to the Word of God. For it is written..." Then I'll finish with a scripture that is applicable to that situation. Usually, my "go to" scripture is 1 Corinthians 10:13 which states:

> *No temptation has overtaken you except such as is common to man; but God is faithful, who will not allow*

you to be tempted beyond what you are able, but with the temptation will also make the way of escape, that you may be able to bear it.

When I first started my journey, I felt like I was saying that hundreds of times a day, but it was absolutely necessary. By speaking to those temptations, I was arresting the thoughts and bringing it into the captivity of the obedience of Christ. This is more common at the start of your journey because the process of renewing your mind is underway, but you still have fresh pornographic and lustful images in your head that the enemy will trigger. As you progress and move forward, he won't have nearly as much ammunition to use against you because the process of renewing your mind has purged those images from your subconscious. By purging those images, I'm referring to removing their sting, or their ability to cause you to stumble. It's rendering their carnal effectiveness useless. It doesn't, however, necessarily mean you will completely forget about them. There are certain things I've forgotten, while there are others that don't seem to want to go away. There are at least 30 women in my past that I've been sexually intimate with. Now, I'm not saying this to brag at all. I'm trying to prove a point. Most of them, I cannot remember their names or what they looked like. Part of this is because some of them were brief, one-night encounters. Part of it is because I've been renewing my mind continually and God has graciously allowed me to forget.

There are certain instances with porn where the images are as fresh and as vibrant as they were the day I first saw them. If I gave into my flesh, I could recall specific details and graphic images. I could, but I won't. The process of renewing my mind has taken away their effectiveness as I mentioned. Even when the enemy tries to plant a thought in my head by triggering an old image from my memory, I rebuke it and move on. It doesn't affect me anymore. It's like a person dying. When someone dies, it stings. It hurts. But, if enough time passes, it doesn't hurt anymore. The sting is gone. Now, knowing that the "sting" has been taken out of these memories is **not** and excuse to dwell on them. That would be utterly foolish. Make no provisions for the flesh or the devil. *Selah.*

Chapter 44: Accountability

Accountability is a big part of being successful. Every man needs to have a Paul, a Barnabas, and a Timothy in his life. I call this the accountability tree. Paul is viewed as the elder statesman – the sage. As a man, you should have an older, wiser man in your life who is more spiritually mature and advanced than you are. You should also give this man authority to speak into your life as someone who can disciple you. This needs to be a man that you both respect and trust. You also need to be confident in his abilities to handle the affairs of his own life such as his marriage, family, job, etc. If there are blatant areas of his life that are lacking, it may be difficult for you to receive from him when it's necessary. Sure, he's a good provider and is faithful to his wife, but if he's a lousy father because he spends too much time at work, maybe he's not the best person to be giving you life advice. Jesus is our ultimate example, but it's helpful to have earthly examples as well. As the Apostle Paul said, "Follow me, as I follow Christ."

Barnabas is seen as your equal. This is someone who is closer in age who you would consider to be at a similar stage in his life. He is someone who is on your level as it relates to your faith. This is a more balanced relationship. This is the iron sharpening iron relationship. This is someone who could help you one day and need your help the next. Because he has similar struggles as you do at this point in his life, it's easier to be open and honest without the fear or worry of disappointing him.

Timothy is a person that you can be a mentor to. He's like your disciple. After all, Jesus called us to make disciples. He doesn't necessarily have to be physically younger than you, but in order for the relationship to work the way it should, he should be less spiritually mature than you are. Regardless of where you are as it relates to your relationship with God and your spiritual maturity, there is always someone who could use you as an example. Having someone in your life that looks up to you is a good form of accountability because it makes you watch your steps. If someone else is watching you to be their example, you're going to be more careful about the decision you make, right?

This form of accountability works for both men and women, but your accountability partners should be of the same sex. So, if you're a man you shouldn't have women in your accountability tree, and if you're a woman you shouldn't have men. This isn't referring to your spouse, but I'll get in to that later. This accountability works for all areas of your life, not just your sexual purity. As it relates to internet accountability, I recommend Covenant Eyes (www.covenanteyes.com). It provides accountability reports to your partner about questionable internet sites that you've visited. It also takes it a step further that other accountability programs by blocking and filtering pornographic sites. In addition it gives sites ratings like Teen, Mature, Highly Mature, etc which make it easier for your accountability partner(s) to review the reports. Covenant Eyes also allows multiple accountability partners, and they can go to the website and run an accountability report for you at any time. The thing I like most is that Covenant Eyes requires you to download an uninstall code from the website before you can remove the program from your computer. Generating that code also sends an e-mail notification to your accountability partner(s). They also had mobile apps for your smart phones and tablets that will link to your account. It's pretty sweet. The filtering and accountability together cost about $10 a month. Because Covenant Eyes has been such a blessing to me and my wife during this journey, I decided to partner with them by becoming an affiliate. I was able to secure a free 1-month trial for all of my readers by using the coupon code **JRICE** at checkout. I hope that this service will bless you the way that it has blessed me.

If you are married, I believe that your spouse should be part of this healing process. That sound you hear right now is all of the married men grumbling. Yes, I said it, and I truly believe it. There are those who feel that spouses should be "spared" the pain of this process, but in actuality, I think the porn user is the one who wants to be spared the discomfort of a questioning spouse. I'll be the first to admit that having a woman in your life who knows about your history will make you very uncomfortable initially. Though your primary sin is against God, you are sinning against your spouse as well, and that's why I believe that they should be involved in this process. Now, does that mean that you have to tell her every dirty little detail? Not necessarily. This is where you need to use wisdom. You also need to talk to her up front and find out what she's comfortable with. You may have to adjust things after you've had some time to put them into practice. For example, let's say you saw an attractive woman who was dressed with the sole intention of luring your eyes. Without intentionally looking for it, you notice that her thong is sticking out above her pants. Even if you rebuke that image and pray to God for strength, chances are your flesh will start talking to you – at least in the beginning of your journey. Despite the fact that you may have won that battle, telling your wife that another woman's thong was pulling on your flesh may cause her pain. She's wired differently than you are, and may never fully understand what you're going through. This is an opportunity for you to simply say, "Hunnie, the devil tried to tempt me today and I rebuked him." If she asked you specifics, you can tell her that another woman was dressed a certain way and it was tempting to look, but you resisted the second glance. If she further persists, you need to warn her that it may be difficult for her to hear and be sure that she wants to know. If at that point she still wants to know and she's hurt by what she hears, she brought it on herself. That's something that she has to learn and an area that she maybe needs to mature and develop. Some people are just nosey and want to know every dirty little detail. Again, the idea here is using wisdom.

In the beginning of my journey, Jess used to follow up and check up on me everyday. There were times where the things I revealed to her were painful. After a while she stopped asking me everyday. Now, she checks in on me occasionally and just asks me if I've had any struggles recently or if the enemy has tried to tempt me. If there's anything to report, I'm open and honest. If not, I let her know. Despite the fact that I've been porn free for a couple years now, she still holds me accountable. And that's very important because sexual purity is an essential part of a marriage partnership.

There's also the fear factor. I've always been taught that fear is a great motivator. Now, the Bible says that God has not given us a spirit of fear, but of power, and of love and of a sound mind. This means that our lives should not be run or dictated by fear. However, I think in certain situations, small doses are fear can be productive and helpful motivators. For example, I'm afraid of how bad it would hurt my wife for me to fall back into porn that it's one of my motivating factors to stay on track. I'm not afraid of heights, but I respect the law of gravity enough not to lean too far over my balcony railing. Does that make sense? When I was a child, my fear of my father's belt kept me in line....most of the time. I guess fear when it's defined as respect or reverence is good, but when it's a debilitating kind of terror then it's not.

Chapter 45: The Day the Devil Calls

If you follow the steps that I've laid out in this book, you will be successful. Like any kind of behavioral change, overcoming a porn addiction takes some time. The change in your heart is instantaneous, but the change in your habits and behavior needs to be developed. Again, the first forty days are definitely the hardest. That's when you'll have the most challenges. Not only will the enemy be working against your success, but your flesh, the traitor within, will also be fighting tooth and nail against you. This is the time to put all you've learned into practice. Remember, God gave us our sex drive, but he also gave us his Word steer the drive and brakes to help control it. Your car has ABS brakes. As it relates to cars, ABS stands for anti-lock braking system. We too have ABS brakes for our purity. ABS = Arrest your thoughts, Bounce your eyes, and Starve your flesh. In the beginning, these practices take time and effort. After a while, they become second nature. If you accidentally touch something hot, you don't have to think about it to make yourself jerk your hand back. It's a natural reaction. Eventually, that's how you'll respond to temptations and opportunities to be tempted. If my eyes happen to come across something sensual, whether it's a scantly clad woman on TV or in the grocery store, my eyes bounce away out of habit. I don't even have to think about it anymore because it's a natural reaction.

This may be the most important thing I have to say in this book: do not allow small victories in small battles to cause you to lose the bigger war. And what I mean is, enjoy your success, but keep pressing forward. Keep striving to improve, and never settle for the progress that's been made. The ace in the hole that the devil will undoubtedly play is complacency. Many people show progress and success for days, weeks, months, and even years only to drop their guards and get blindsided back to square one. You have to keep doing what you did to become successful and can't take your foot off the gas once you think you've made enough progress. Trust me on this one.

I live in Maryland where Interstate 70 starts. I-70 actually ends all the way in Cove Fort, Utah. I remember coming from Baltimore and getting on I-70 one day, right at its beginning. I noticed a big green sign that listed locations and their distances from that particular point. This sign, however, was different than any I had ever seen before. Instead of listing upcoming and nearby locations, it listed destinations quite a ways away.

Columbus – 420 miles
St. Louis – 840 miles
Denver – 1700 miles
Cove Fort – 2200 miles

I have always found that odd. Why would they be advertising destinations that far away? Then one day at church, my pastor brought up that very topic. He said that our actions and our behaviors are just like that road sign. We tend to live in the moment, not thinking about where we're going. We don't have the foresight to see where we'll end up by traveling on a particular path. In essence, that sign was telling me, if you stay on the path you're on right now, you'll hit Columbus, Ohio in 420 miles. If you don't change your course at all, this is where you'll end up. The same is true for the other destinations. This concept should be applied to our behavior and our habits. When you make subtle compromises as it relates to your purity, you are taking steps in the wrong direction. You're embarking on a path that leads you to a place you don't want to end up.

There are a few things that you need to keep in mind. Sexual purity is not a destination. It is a journey. There's never a point where you can just throw your hands in the air and shout, "I've done it! I'm finished!" I'm sorry, but it just doesn't work that way. This is a path that you have to choose to continually walk. Looking at this as a destination is a trap the enemy wants you to step into. Have you ever seen someone lose a ton of weight and gain it all back? This happens because people set a goal, and once they reach that goal they stop doing the things they did to get them there. As it relates to your sexual purity, that kind of attitude will set you back so fast it'll make your head spin. Don't get me wrong, there are definitely milestones that need to be celebrated, but don't allow those milestones to cause you to lose sight of the big picture. Specifically, don't loosen your restrictions after you've had success. I don't care if you've been clean a month or a year, you still need to do what you did to get there. I've heard stories from tons of guys who were free from porn for years who fell back into the habit because they didn't keep their guards up. They thought that they could loosen their restrictions by canceling their Covenant Eyes subscription only to find out that the enemy was there all along waiting for them to do something so foolish. When you've been porn free and walking in sexual purity, it's hard to imagine diving back into a porn habit. In that situation, looking at porn seems like miles away, but with every subtle compromise you make, you're taking one step closer. You're pushing those lines and boundaries further and further. Remember, St. Louis was 840 miles away, but if I kept driving in that direction, I'd be there in about 12 hours (it would probably be 10 if my wife was driving).

Picture your purity as a boat keeping you afloat in a sea of temptation. When you first start this journey, your boat is a rickety wooden raft that can barely float on its own, let alone in the turbulence of a sexual hurricane. But everyday you implement these strategies of success, your boat gets bigger and stronger. The seas stay the same because the times we live in aren't going to change. But, as your boat gets bigger and stronger it becomes better equipped to handle the challenge. After a year or so, your boat is a titanic-like cruise ship that is so massive everyday waves and ocean movements don't phase it. Even really bad storms can barely shake its confidence. The only real danger is the iceberg of complacency. Complacency allows us to drop our guards. It allows us to drive staring in the rearview mirror as opposed to focusing on the objects in front of us. When we spend too much attention looking back at our success, we can't be fully prepared for what's coming ahead. Then, all of a sudden we scrape our hulls up against a huge iceberg.

You've been clean for some time now, and proud of your success. But instead of doing what you did to get there, you loosen up. You used to screen every movie for content ahead of time to avoid nudity and sexual situations; now you go to the movies unprepared and get caught by a steamy encounter. Granted, it's not *technically* porn, but your flesh doesn't know the difference. You put yourself in a situation where there's some buxom beauty on screen taking her clothes off. You've traded the no-name porn star for the A-list Hollywood starlet, but the outcome is the same. Your flesh soaks it up. It starts to indulge and consume the images you give it, regardless of how brief or unassuming. Scrape, scrape, scrape. You notice right away that something is wrong. You felt that impact, but it didn't seem life-changing. The world didn't stop spinning. This is Holy Spirit trying to get your attention. He will convict you of your wrongdoings, but the more your feed your flesh, the less and less you hear His voice. You try and justify things in your head because you didn't masturbate. Heck, you hardly got aroused, so it couldn't have been that bad, right? You don't recognize that you're taking on water. The leak is slow and steady, and your descent is subtle. Even worse, you've wet the appetite of destruction that you've spent so long trying to starve.

> *And do this, knowing the time, that now it is high time to awake out of sleep; for now our salvation is nearer than when we first believed. The night is far spent, the day is at hand. Therefore let us cast off the works of darkness, and let us put on the armor of light. Let us walk properly, as in the day, not in revelry and drunkenness, not in lewdness and lust, not in strife and envy. But put on the Lord Jesus Christ, **and make no provision for the flesh, to fulfill its lusts.***
> Romans 13:11-14

The Bible clearly tells us not to make *any* provisions for our flesh to fulfill its lusts. God understands how our flesh works. If you give it *anything* it will consume it and want more, even if it doesn't appear to you like it's something *that* bad. Remember, lust can never be quenched. It is *never* satisfied; so the small, subtle changes you've made to accommodate your flesh are only building up its appetite. Remember when you were a kid and you'd ask your parents to stay up late, just this once? If they let you do it, you undoubtedly used that one time incident as a precedent for future requests. When you asked them in the future and they declined, you pointed back to that one time and said, "But you let me do it last time! Why can't I do it again?" If your parents didn't have any backbone, they probably caved. When you go camping, there's a reason for the sign that says "Do not feed the bears." Because once you do, they will keep coming back. Well, your flesh operates under the same principles. When you give it just a taste, it will come back for more. It will beg. It will plead. It will demand. You try to deny. You try to refuse, but the precedent has been set, and your flesh will point back to the delicious meal of breasts and thighs you fed it the other day and insist on seconds. This is a pivotal moment in your life. If you don't hold firm right now, all of your hard work will have been in vain because giving in to your flesh the second time opens the door for a pattern. The first time was bad, but the second time is much worse because you're telling your flesh, the devil, and all of his minions that this wasn't a one-time lapse in judgment. You're telling them that you are willing to be ensnared again. This was no accident. This was a conscious decision on your part. Your ship is taking on massive amounts of water, and you're well on your way to a re-kindled addiction. A while ago, the destination you're rapidly approaching seemed so far away. Now, it's the next exit. Do you really want to end up there again?

I caution you against this, because it has happened to me. I was two plus years into my deliverance when I started making subtle compromises: letting my eyes linger too long, watching TV shows and movies I shouldn't have, and allowing my mind to wander without restraints. It's amazing (not in a good way) how you can spend years doing the right thing, and a few moments of weakness can undo almost of the progress it took you years to achieve. Think about an alcoholic. Years of sobriety can be flushed down the toilet by one decision to drink. Our deliverance works the same way. I never went back to porn or masturbation, but I definitely crossed the line by deliberately watching some things that I know I shouldn't have.

When God told me to write this book, I was afraid. Not only did I think that the book would be a challenge, but I was concerned about my own purity. I knew that people would look up to me as an example, and I didn't know if I could handle that kind of pressure. Disappointing God and my wife was bad enough. Letting down all of those who read my book and looked up to me would be adding insult to injury. So, I prayed. I prayed that God exposed me quickly and early on, in the event that I started walking down the wrong path. Thankfully, God answers prayers. One morning, Jess caught me viewing some images that I had no business looking at. Again, it wasn't technically porn, but that's a moot point. My intentions were to indulge my flesh, so the fact that there was no nudity is irrelevant. All of the trust that I had worked so hard for had gone down the drain, and I was back at square one with my wife. It was a very humbling experience, but it was necessary. I learned first-hand the dangers of complacency and making subtle compromises. That misstep allowed me to re-evaluate my life, adjust my priorities, and re-focus on what's important. So believe me when I say that you don't want to walk down that path again. Please, I'm begging you. Learn from my mistakes, and don't make them for yourself.

It's a slow fade when you give yourself away
It's a slow fade when black and white have turned to gray
Thoughts invade, choices are made, a price will be paid
When you give yourself away
People never crumble in a day

The journey from your mind to your hands
Is shorter than you're thinking
Be careful if you think you stand
You just might be sinking

Casting Crowns – Slow Fade

Chapter 46: The Call to Arms

So that's it. Our time together has come to a close. You've completed basic training and are ready to go to battle. This book has provided you with all of the information that you need to be successful. If you apply these principles, you will soon enjoy the freedom that has seemed unattainable for so long. Resist the urge to be selfish with your success. There will be others in your life that will need your supply. Remember, God calls us to make disciples. You never know who God will place in your life to help along the way, but it must first begin with your decision to slay this giant.

But Jesus looked at them and said to them, "With men this is impossible, but with God all things are possible."
Matthew 19:26

16604813R00103

Made in the USA
Charleston, SC
31 December 2012